RED DUST 2
New Writing

Babette Sassoon
SACRIFICES
and
GREEN

Simon Vestdijk
MY BROWN FRIEND

Alan Burns
BUSTER

 RED DUST • NEW YORK

CONTENTS

SACRIFICES
and
GREEN

BABETTE SASSOON

SACRIFICES

There was no more terrifying place to Austin than Crispin's garden, for everything that grew in it seemed to the child to express the gardener's craziness. The lawn so green and complacent that stretched in front of the house held shadows in its sod, the trunk of the oak tree at the end of the lawn was carved out with age; Austin had stood in it one day and trembling with terror had imagined how Crispin, ever on the look out for him, might find him there and slide in beside him, his long arms twisting like oak worms about Austin's chest, his feet planted firmly in the roots, till Crispin and the tree wriggled into one mass and the sap rose into the leaves frothing from Austin's veins. In the rock garden water slithered over lapis stones and moss, trickled through blue bells and lady slippers, hung on the algae. Over its gurgle he could hear Crispin's crackling footsteps. Shaking with anticipation he pretended indifference, looked ostentatiously in the other direction, kept a sharp eye out lest he be suddenly pounced upon unawares, chucked under the chin, tickled in the ribs, or held in the air by his heels for a dizzying minute while, the blood rushing to his head, he viewed the garden, bird-like, swinging in Crispin's grip. Running away he longed to catch him. "If only once I could do the pouncing, he'd disappear into thin air." He imagined himself a huge black bird that fell flapping on Crispin's shoulders and with the immense span of his wings flattened Crispin into the earth. Casually hopping on one foot and head in the air Austin started out in the direction of the rock garden. Crispin would not stay there long, it was in his nature that he should skulk behind trees. They were tall enough to camouflage his gaunt frame and long skinny arms whose fingers poked deep into the earth, transplanted weeds into a patch of their own, having decided that nothing should die before its time. His silhouette gyrated ridiculously in the shadow's. Austin knew that if Crispin was in the orchard which stretched in back of the house beginning with the rock garden, flying up a hill and into the horizon and circling back to the side door of the pantry by the vegetable plot, the game would end horribly. The prospect of Crispin hiding amongst a hundred tree trunks was enough to terrify Austin out of his assumed indifference. His step as light as possible, his sight straining for jerky movements, his ears shutting out all but the unnatural sounds, he moved like a hunter.

"Crispin! I see you! Come out!" he called, thrusting his words like antennae into the orchard. He was lost among the indistinguishable apple trees. There the weeds grew tall. Dandelions became huge puffs. Queen Anne's lace hung like suspended snow.

"Crispin! I know where you are!" he cried.

Once Austin had overheard his mother telling his father that Crispin should be dismissed. Hearing his father's refusal he had been both alarmed at the immutability of Crispin's position and relieved that the victory over the gardener was not to be snatched from him.

"He is weak minded" his mother said in the imperious tone she always used. "He is bad for the child. God knows what crazy ideas he will put into his head."

"He has nowhere to go." Mr. Carver said.

"What has that to do with me? I'm not running a vet's shop here. Have you ever seen his room?"

"I don't see what harm it could do anyone. It's in the basement anyway."

"It's a disgrace, an ungodly disgrace."

"What difference can it make if he wishes to keep maimed animals?"

"When an animal is maimed its own species destroys it and when a plant grows crooked it wilts before bearing seed and that is God's plan."

"Crispin has nowhere to go."

"You know what he wants don't you? He wants to lure Austin into his room, my child, in the middle of that unnatural, broken refuse."

"He has nowhere to go. He grew up here. This place belongs to him as much as to us. When my father hired him what is now the garden was pasture and woods. At fifteen years old Crispin cleared the land, he dug out the rock..."

"Even the rocks he would not throw away."

"My father humored him. I can still hear Crispin stuttering out his case for the rocks: 'They will lie one on top of the other and keep each other warm,' and he built a wall..."

"Off the property. It's useless."

10

"Thanks to him we have the orchard..."

"I loathe the orchard. It makes my house look like a farmhouse."

"He saved the oak tree..."

"The oak tree is dying."

"He will save it."

"Is he trying to save Austin too?"

"Whatever from?"

"Don't you mean, whoever from?"

"Austin is yours, you know that."

"Crispin is carrying on with Amy. I'd love to know what goes on at night in the basement. He revolts me. Perhaps he's not as crazy as you think. When I give him an order and he just looks into space and starts stammering out a long stupid monologue on some quite different subject..."

"You give him impossible orders. You know very well the orchard can't be cut down..."

"Why not? Why should we produce barrels of apples just for Crispin's satisfaction?"

"We could always sell them..."

"I'd rather they rotted."

"I wish you could have seen the first time the orchard bloomed when the trees were still small, quite near the ground, the tiniest whitest flowers over the brown furrows like transparent seed pearls."

Though Mrs. Carver could not get rid of Crispin she did her best to annihilate the impact of his paganism. From within herself she squeezed out every drop of derision until the household noticed that Mrs. Carver who seldom laughed, laughed till her sides ached at Crispin's occupancy of the basement room. When winter came she announced that Crispin as surely as his own bulbs and roots was imprisoned underground. She likened the parquet floor to the frozen earth under which Crispin, along with all paraphenalia of summer, lay hopelessly trapped. Even the spring evoked from her a recital of how Crispin, his bony frame panting to wriggle out of its grave, would emerge bit by ridiculous bit, an ungainly presence amongst the tender and pastel crocuses.

"Daffy down dilly back again" said Austin and Mrs. Carver added,

"Crazy man, his hair is grass, his feet are pods, crazy man sees nothing at all for his eyes are seeds, his ears are leaves, his throat

11

is a long rough stem and no sense comes out of it, and his nose is no nose at all, his nose is a sharpened sickle."

"Daffy down dilly has come home again!"

"Home, child?"

"Yes Mother. Home, to the garden."

"But", she said, closing the front door. "He has no home. And that is why he is different from us."

"How is he different?"

"You remember. You say it." She held his small hands in her own, and between each phrase encouraged his memory with her assenting pleasure.

"He talks he-he- el- ooo..."

"Oh yes" she laughed exageratedly.

"O -o-o...stin!"

"Oh wonderful..."

"Would y-y-you l-like a p-p-posy?"

"Not too fast, not so fast." she gloated.

When he was very little, he sometimes woke up sweating in the middle of the night. In the strangeness of the hour his training forsook him. Confusing his mother with the terrifying eye of God from which there was no escape he slid down the chute of heretical prayers.

"Dear God, I do not thank you for my good home with its strong walls which keep out the wind, I do not thank you for the roof which keeps my pillow dark, I do not thank you for not making me a tree which has no choice where it will stand, I do not thank you for not making me a bird whose only thought is food, I do not thank you for making me a human being ...and...I wish..." he whispered into the sheets..."I wish I was crazy man Crispin."

Daytimes his common sense reassured him there were more advantages to being Austin Carver than a tree, a blade of grass, a wild animal, a zinnia. If sometimes Crispin filled him with delicious and sensual horror he still rendered up the dutiful echo of his mother's laughter.

Although he had never given her cause to pit her anger against him, he was in constant terror that one day her fury would annihilate him as it had his father that terrible morning when she found out how for a month father and son, sneaking off together, had nearly succeeded in betraying her.

For it was his father whom he scarcely knew, who had up to now seemed to shun him, who never heard his prayers or played with him, who had invented this plot whereby they spent the month close in each other's company. Every day after school they were absent for more than two hours. At Mrs. Carver's questions they only smiled. Austin delighted in the daily visits to the art studio, playing with the long brushes whose colored ends stippled lovely designs on paper, or watching the form of his father growing on the white canvas, his arm around his son. His father played marvelous games, his father laughed all the time and never scolded and if he had not been so shy he might have joined in the evening prayers, have tucked him in bed, have told him stories. The painting was a birthday present for Mrs. Carver. At last the eve of the great day arrived. All that night Austin was in a fever of expectancy, terrified lest his mother should guess anything.

Early next morning his father woke him up; together they slipped into her room and at the foot of the bed they placed on an easel the portrait, now magnificently framed in gilded oak. Hours seemed to pass while they waited anxiously for her to wake up. Mr. Carver was drinking his fifth cup of tea. Suddenly there burst through the house a hysterical scream, high and animalish sounding, and then the thudding of something falling down the stairs. He turned blotched white when he heard his wife's shriek, holding the cup to his lips with a paralyzed arm; abruptly he let it drop and rushed to the stairway. At his feet the painted likeness of his son stared at him upside down. His own face she had ripped with a pair of scissors. He lurched at the sight as if the blade had entered his flesh and turned to grasp the banister. Slipping on the edge of the frame he fell to his knees. Mrs. Carver appeared at the top. She looked at her husband with glittering composure then, calling her son, watched while he skirted his father's body which seemed to him crouched there permanently.

In her bedroom she spoke to Austin with a solicitude which until that moment had never been so tender. It was her tone more than her words which convinced the child of his disloyalty, the anguish in her voice which proved to him that the union the father had aimed for would have excluded her. When, purged and confessed, he descended to the drawing room and saw his father sitting alone with his head in his hands and met the grief filled glance a sudden instinct of self preservation led him coldly from the room.

He was the center of the world, her tone implied. He meant so much to her that she would die if he were absent from her; he was the emperor of love and had never known it, he was love itself, he had no faults, he was a divine child. "I shall not be afraid of Crispin any longer" he thought, "I shall pounce on him." but wary still, he thought he had better start with Amy.

Amy was prettier and far younger than his mother and sometimes while he sat at the supper table in the kitchen he caught her looking at herself in the mirror above the sink. Then he too craned his neck to get a glimpse of the blonde hair, the round pink face, the brown eyes he had jealously detected becoming soft at the sight of Crispin and, twisting at the table to get a better view, he turned over the wobbly stool. Amy turned on him, her expression contemptuous, her fist raised. "What's wrong with mother's little darling?" she screamed. "Isn't he eating his kidneys? What's he staring at the cook for? What would mother say about little darling demeaning himself? Little tittle tattle had to run and tell her all about the food Amy cooks for Crispin as if it didn't have enough with its artichokes and cucumber soups. Poor little darling is starving to death and wants Crispin's food too." She sing songed all over the kitchen, "Mother's little darling, Mother's little darling!" Austin's embarrassment was increased by the certainty that if his mother had walked into the kitchen at that moment, she would not have noticed that anything was amiss.

He had to take matters into his own hands. Five o'clock one afternoon a stiff, poker faced, glaring Austin entered the Kitchen, his tie knotted extra tight, knees scrubbed, nails scraped with the large blade of his pocket knife, hair plastered on his forehead, an expression the haughtiness of which he had practiced all day behind the locked bathroom door. He regarded Amy straight in the eye for the first time.

"Aren't you the gentleman." she said, startled in spite of herself.

"From now on, to you, I shall be Master Austin." The poise with which he delivered his well rehearsed phrase was lost on neither of them.

"Crispin! Come here!" he called, standing in the vestibule and summoning Crispin into the house for the first time in his life. "Come here!"

"Damn Crispin", Austin thought, feeling very grown up in the silent reverberation of his mother's marvelous expression. "God damn you" he repeated the words which had awakened him late one night. He knew that the door of the room adjoining his mother's was open, otherwise he would not have heard her "damn you" so clearly. He lay in bed, not daring to turn over, a leech, sucking out the energy of her robust curse. He heard slippered steps shuffling up and down the room, accompanied by his father's murmurs. Instinctively he knew that whatever 'damn' meant, it was a cry of triumph. What, anyway, was his father doing in her room? Hadn't she promised when she took his teddy bear away, that all adults slept alone? Hadn't she shown him the key to her room as a proof that she was not just humoring him, and when he found teddy bear in a pile of soup bones and vegetable peelings on the top of the garbage can, hadn't she told him that if he wanted to become an adult he would have to throw into the refuse along with Teddy all his childish notions, the primary one being that there was anyone or anything in the world which could ever, once one grew up, be a solace for what she called the "terrible loneliness of life", and that the sooner he became used to adult loneliness the better? Then what was his father doing in her room? Deep in the night were they breaking the rules? His mother's furious denial burst through the house and long after the door between their room had been slammed, his thoughts echoed her "God damn you".

Amy looked at herself because there was no one else to do it, his father mumbled to himself because no one listened, his mother proclaimed her own virtue because there was no one to laud her. Only Crispin insisted that his flowers engaged in loving conversation with him, that the apple trees just before they burst into blossom whispered all sorts of secrets, that the grass was full of messages, which proved once and for all that Crispin was not a grown up, that in God's world he did not count.

No, Crispin was not lonely. Years after his mother had chased away the three legged kitten Austin discovered it, a huge cat cowering in Crispin's room, rubbing its deformity against him. There was a rose bush so covered with beetles that by mid summer nothing was left but naked twigs and thorns. Rescued by Crispin it bloomed on his window sill. An egg which had fallen out of the nest in the early spring hatched miraculously by the furnace. Amy too, with tidbits of unsuccessful dishes, with hodge podge casseroles of leftovers, with a variety of chipped receptacles, pots, pans, glasses, with all sorts of broken objects conspired to make Crispin cozy. The day Teddy was thrown out Austin, from behind the tomato bushes, held his breath lest he be discovered and watched Crispin swinging him in great circles of laughter, a moldy lettuce leaf hung over one ear.

"Crispin will get old like an animal and never know it." Mrs. Carver said.

Austin could damn him as loud as he pleased, Crispin was likely to spring up right under his nose stammering, "I b-b-beg your p-p-pardon?" several times or "Do e-e-excuse me" in droll mockery of the social phrases Amy had taught him, holding his huge hand cupped to his ear, bowing to the ground. The play acting under which the real man masqueraded, as if waiting to be detected, made Austin uncomfortable. He had no wish to be acquainted with the real Crispin. When his mother gave Crispin orders, Austin never missed the false obeisance with which he smiled too broadly and nodded too often, only to look bored the next instant, eyes focused on the horizon, a sigh escaping him so audibly that, shaking his head as if shocked by his own behavior, his attention swooped back on Mrs. Carver who, her lips pursed, ordered him to weed out all the daffodils. As he doffed his hat in extravagant imitation of a courtly gesture and murmured "your will be done" he imagined his mother speaking, not to the gardener, but to a spirit which refused all authority but its own, an unknown soul which demanded that the exploratory fingers of camraderie, concern, and even love pick off its brown husk.

Austin bolstered himself with visions of hell. Every day the angels, leaning over balconies of pink clouds, their wings fluttering and their laughter bubbling, would view the telescoped grotesqueries being performed, light years away in the illuminated pit below. Crispin, in his fiery circus, with a hundred mimicking shadows like paper cutouts crisped at the edges would tumble ludicrously by. Looking up at the merciless snickers he would pray that his bony frame might desist from its senseless salaaming, that his arm might pause in its nonsensical hat doffing, that his tongue might miss, if only once its regular, "excuse me, oh excuse me, oh I beg your p-p-pardon". God, who wished heaven to be entertained, would never hear his appeal. His limbs would twitch forever, his features would be punkered regularly in monstrous ticks, his fingers would itch and under his nails vines and bushes would scrape his skin; beneath his rubs sharp eyed birds would make their nests; in his hair insects would tunnel a haven; in the crook of his arm a squirrel would plant an acorn from which a gigantic tree would sprout instantly, and pulled asunder by its strength, Crispins's soul would burst into flames.

"Come here, you damn Crispin" Austin cried, unwilling to go into the garden after him. Banging the front door he stood behind it out of breath with rage. Suddenly the door opened, hit him in the face, and trapped him against the wall. Austin closed his eyes and covered his face with his hands. In dreadful anxiety he looked around the door and was presented with an extraordinary sight. Crispin. Crispin peering down the hall, squinting at the darkness. Crispin craning his neck round the corner of the drawing room, about to vandalize with his presence its shady tenderness, the plush cleanliness of its Persian rugs. Austin whipped around the door and crashed into Crispin who burst into raucous laughter which he immediately made elaborate attempts to stifle.

"What are you doing in the house?"

"T-t-trying to b-b-breathe" Crispin said, between bouts of guffaws.

"What are you up to?"

"How f-f-funny for you to ask me, you of all p-p-people to ask me of all p-p-people. What is it you're up t-to?"

"Me"

"Hiding b-b-behind the door. Trying to scare the household? a l-l-little one like you. Trying to play b-b-bogey man?"

"You're not supposed to be in the hallway."

"You n-n-neither."

"What do you mean? This is my house, you crazy man."

"Would you like to run a-a-away?"

"Crazy thing."

"Bogey b-b-baby in the dark house. Why do you spend the day stuffed in the attic?"

"You know why you talk so silly?"

"Why? b-b-bogey b-b-bird?"

"Because you have no mind and soon you're going to die."

"And how about you, l-l-little b-b-bogey brain, you going to l-l-live forever?"

"You're going to die sometime very soon."

"We could be b-b-buried together, Austy Wausty."

"Don't call me that."

"What? Austy Wausty? D-d-don't c-c-call you Austy Wausty? I c-c-call you Austy Wausty b-b-because I love you."

"Do you think I care if someone like you loves me."

"Aren't you the young fool. Don't even know that no one else l-l-loves you. Don't go r-r-round throwing away the only tiny bit of l-l-love you'll ever get.

17

"The only reason that I waited for you in the ..."

"So you were h-h-hiding."

"Was to give you this piece of information. From now on you are to call me Master Austin."

"What does that s-s-silly thing m-m-mean?"

"What thing?"

"Info - what? Infomat? What does that m-m-mean, Austy Wausty Stinny Winny?"

"What I am saying..."

"Oh, I b-b-beg your pardon."

"From now on you must call me Master Austin."

"But, l-l-little one, of course, I know your name. It's only b-b-because I love you that I make l-l-little changes in it."

"Master. That's what I said, Master."

"I hear."

"Then say it."

"Say what, l-l-little one?"

"Say Master."

"Master, O.K. All you have to d-d-do is ask Crispin for your heart's d-d-desire."

"Say Master Austin, not just Master by itself, but Austin too."

"Austin, O.K.?"

"Master Austin."

"Poor l-l-little man, gets so e-e-excited."

"Amy calls me Master Austin."

"Oh, that's a good one, a g-g-good one, well, little b-b-bogey I'm off. I'll just g-g-go in the kitchen and see if Amy's there. I'll t-t-tell her what you said. Oh, it's a g-g-good one."

"Say, I'm off, Master Austin."

But Crispin had already disappeared down the hall through the kitchen door. Austin tiptoed up to it and with his ear pressed at the keyhole heard Crispin's laughter as he repeated over and over, his stutter and giggles intermingling in a breathless jargon,

"I think I'll just say K-K-King Carver, King C-C-Carver, King Carver..."

"King Carver" Amy, breathless too, repeated, "Oh, that's just great."

"King Carver?" Austin mused, rolling the words on his tongue, wondering if they did not sound even grander than Master Austin. And he envisioned himself King of the World on a throne so high that only his mother would from time to time be able to ascend, so massive that all the ghostly trees of all the forests place end to end would be dwarfed at its pedestal, so bright that even the night would cast no shadows.

II

Valery sat on the sofa beside Austin staring into space. He pressed her hand. She didn't move. She looked anesthetized. She let him play with her fingers. "Talk to me" he said.

"Alright" Her voice was almost a whisper. Her voice was as expressionless as her face.

"Tell me you like me."

"I like you."

Never mind, he thought, she will. She was exactly what he had envisioned, fragile, pale, golden haired, low voiced, gentle, young. He had waited for her all his life, luminous eyes under a snowy forehead, inviolate in a fluted dress. Terrestrial and lustful, he crouched below. In a frenzy of imagination he pursued the dream to its apex, the miracle from which his father had been excluded. I will find her one day, not even noticing how middle age was coming on him, she will save me.

In his adolescent poems the miracle always occurred. The frigid lids trembled, the stone eyes filled with pity, sympathy bridged the gap, anxiety melted.

Valery sat beside him on the sofa staring at the wall. It's the way of young girls, he said to himself. In the back room he heard her aunt muddling about. She had left them alone for the first time on account of the momentousness of the occasion. A month ago his life had been desolate, now he had before him the prospect of intimacy, someone at his side who, full of gratitude towards him, would love him.

She was on her way from school. She tripped on the sidewalk scattering books and papers. Suddenly she felt insistent hands yanking at her. She struggled against him but he stood rigid above her, unsmiling, old. His eyes glinted as he foolishly raised her to a kneeling position.

"I'm alright" she cried, "Let go."

"No, no, I'll see you home. Your knee is bleeding."

"It's nothing."

"I'll see you home just the same." He had waited too long for this moment to waste it. He gripped her arm. She clenched her fist. When they reached the house he went up the steps with her, he rang the bell before she could get her keys.

"She has hurt herself" he announced to the old woman who finally answered the door. "She fell down and now her knee is bleeding."

The old woman turned an amazed and sly glance at Valery. "It was lucky that I happened to be walking by" Austin said.

"I'm alright" Valery said helplessly. He was asked in, offered a cup of coffee. He sat on the edge of the worn sofa he was destined to know so well in the coming month and while the girl was sent upstairs to wash up the woman sat opposite Austin. He learned from her that Valery was an orphan, that in another month she would finish school and have to find a job. "Though heaven knows who will give her a job, they teach them so little in school these days. When I was her age I was already taking in sewing and helping out."

"I suppose it worries you?" Austin asked absently, noting the paucity of furniture, the dingy wallpaper. She would be grateful to be taken out of this, he thought dreamily, waiting for to come down.

"Valery, you come down" the aunt called out.

"Valery, what a lovely name."

"Valery" he murmured through the coming weeks when he came daily to call on her. Aunt Maude posted herself opposite them, glued to her eternal sewing.

"Valery", his eyes gleamed and his fingers inched their way along the edge of the couch.

"Valery, Valery" he went stubbornly and stupidly on and on till at last she didn't even listen. Her aunt watched like a stage manager to be sure that Valery, whose hair she had taken to vigorously brushing and whose dresses she had gone to the trouble of personally pressing, gave full satisfaction. Every afternoon Valery hoped: Today will be the last of him. It was inconceivable that he should keep returning with his flowers and candies and gifts of handkerchiefs and hair ribbons which she left wilting and unopened on the stained coffee table in front of him. Soon she would have a job and be unavailable.

"He wants to marry you." Aunt Maude announced. "He's not coming today. To give you time."

"Time for what?"

"Don't be an idiot."

When he came by that morning Aunt Maude could tell right away by his constrained expression what was up. He sat on the edge of the sofa, the inevitable cup of coffee trembling in his hand.

"I want to marry her. I'll give her everything she could ever want. She'll have no worries. I'll be more than husband to her. I'll keep her close and safe, she'll have nothing to do. On the day of our marriage I'll give you a pension."

But Valery pouted "I won't marry him, Aunt Maude, you know I won't."

"He adores you. You'll wrap him around your little finger. And anyway I don't see you have a choice."

"I won't do it."

"You will. Something like this will never come our way again. It's a miracle. It's settled."

In the silence, of the next afternoon they sat alone for the first time, though Austin did not kiss her. Staring noncommitally into space she gave no sign of recognizing her new status in his life and despite the aunt's assurances he was beginning to doubt his luck when the old lady suddenly came in and relieved his uncertainty with the news she had lost no time in getting to work on the wedding dress. "Try it on" she said sharply. Valery obeyed. He was overjoyed. She might wear the most deadpan expression and have not once smiled at him but she had a good as shouted her assent when he consented to try on the dress sewn into which he would finally possess her.

He repeated her name, in a voice edged with sudden impatience, "I thee take". On her finger he plunged the wedding band with violent awkwardness. A few moments later they stood on the church steps. He looked down at her with eyes bright as the candles on the altar at which she had been obliged to kneel. She felt, before turning away, his inquisitive fingers nagging at her hair which, at his strange request, hung loose down her back and his clammy palm propelling her cheek towards him. Then, it dawned on her, the enormity of her task, to keep her soul inviolate from him.

Her veil screened her cheek. About her feet the bridal train twisted its ridiculous length. His eyes took in the pleasing folds of her dress with possessive satisfaction and in that gratified glance of ownership she saw the scheme of things to come.

She stood at the window of the hotel room he had engaged for their honeymoon, hugging to her heart not her innocence but her repugnance. She felt the longing of his uncertain and synthetic touch. Feigning exhaustion she held herself as still as death.

As soon as he had closed the door and she saw with what care he was amassing the little bits of colored paper which clung to his clothes, she opened the window wide and they flew from his hand.

Then she removed the burdensome head gear with its uncomfortable veil and dumped in on the floor.

"You will have everything the way you like it." he said timidly, "You will be the mistress of my house." He opened his arms as if at this generous announcement she should have rushed into his embrace. She looked at him with the vague expression of a very young girl who cannot possibly make out the actions of her elders.

"I shouldn't think you'd want anything changed." she said at last.

"Why do you suppose I married you, Valery?" he answered.

III

She gulped, tears welled up, she blinked and they overflowed, hung on her lashes and coursed down her cheeks. But under their watery shells her eyes were sly.

Determined to touch her he struck her. If his caresses got no response at least his slap drew from her a startled shriek. She recovered long before him. In a rage he sent her out of the room. She obeyed quickly, almost skipping.

Sitting on a stool by the desk Valery watched her husband's writing, loops and dots over the pages of the account book he was trying to teach her how to keep. Every time he handed her the pen she made some stupid mistake, added the simplest sums incorrectly, multiplied the date by the groceries, wrote the month in the expense column. Relying on his temper she jerked her arm and overturned the ink bottle. He gripped her wrist so hard that through the tightened skin the veins swelled blue and the knuckles, from which the fingers dangled paralyzed, glistened. Under his middle finger the wrist bone protruded invitingly, her pulse fluttered in his palm. His hand crashed down on hers. He watched his child bride rush from the room thinking, at least I have touched her.

He sat alone before the ink splattered account book he cared nothing about, feeling lightheaded. If I followed her to her room I'd only find her nestled comfortably in the pillows. He would not count on her contrition.

Austin said, "You do as you wish with her house. Now it's yours. Muddy up the rugs, pull the curtains open, do anything you like. Create any havoc you like. And in the place of her portrait will hang yours."

When Austin, to her great relief, deciding that their month's honeymoon should be cut short, brought her home and carried her jestingly over the threshold, she unconsciously added to the joke by sticking out her feet so that he could not manage to get her through the narrow front door without the most ridiculous shoving and sidling and when she fell out of his arms and landed in the darkness of the hallway, she saw through a tiny window under the staircase the apple trees tinselled with buds in the May sun. Austin pulled her into the dining room. Mrs. Carver's stylized features under silver hair regarded her daughter-in-law out of a background of towers, turrets, and spires. Austin demanded her reaction with a nervous smile.

"It's a wonderful picture!" Valery said, her voice for the first time joyous. Austin gave a surprised jerk, looked down at her anxiously. She ignored him. Her spontaneous words had nothing to do with him. Her gaze never focused directly on him. Behind her half closed lids he imagined she escaped into vapor, endless space.

"A wonderful picture" she exulted. "It's as if she were still living . . ." full of mirth was her tone. Mrs. Carver's painted eye pursued her with icy approval: Valery's heart lifted in a great surge of unexpected hope.

"I would not have it moved" she said. "I make no claims."

On the rare occasions when she spoke to him at all, uttering monosyllabic trivialities or cutting off endearments with a dull phrase, he realized that from her thin, childish voice, as if by mere contact with himself all youth had vanished. And now he was so filled with wonder at her happy tone he heard not one word she said.

Valery felt his hand, clammy with suspense, circling her neck, bending it towards him. She looked straight ahead, holding her breath, as if she were about to be throttled.

Her gaze switched reluctantly from the painted bosom to the forehead of her husband. His nose grazed her cheek, she looked into his fluttering blue-veined lids and on her lips a cloying dampness settled.

Her frigid innocence exhibited his kiss in all its incompetence. Mrs. Carver watched while he held the unwilling girl close.

"Behind the curtains" Valery said, "Someone's knocking at the window." Her loud laugh startled Austin.

Snatching the curtain aside he saw smack up against Valery's face Crispin's grimacing one. His arms were flapping at his side. Austin pushed Valery aside.

"What's ...the matter?"

"Don't stammer for God's sake Valery...What do you want, Crispin?" Through the pane he saw Crispin's lips stuttering out some long speech. "Can't you see I'm busy?" he shouted, opening the window.

"I j-j-just wanted to w-w-welcome you home, you and the young l-l-lady- the new Mrs. C-C-Carver." Crispin roared with laughter. Valery hurried forward.

"Hello" she said. "You must be the gardener. I've heard all about you."

"We have no time for you now, Crispin. We just arrived."

"I know. I've been watching ag-g-gog for you."

"I can't wait to see the garden" Valery said.

"First you'll see the rest of the house" Austin said and banged the window closed in Crispin's face.

"Why were you so rude to him?"

"It's something between Crispin and me. You wouldn't understand."

"Tell me."

"It's nothing interesting." How explain Crispin's monstrous attitude, how explain that since he was a child it was the idiotic gardener who had tried to drum into Austin, he, Master Austin, that he was the one who was out of place.

"Crispin l-l-loves little Austy W-W-Wausty b-b-because Crispin loves everything c-c-crippled."

"I liked him" Valery said. "He's so funny. I'll get him to take me through the orchard."

"You'll do what I tell you."

"Why...what's wrong?"

"I don't know."

"How long has Crispin been here? Did he really plant the orchard?"

Later, on the occasion of Crispin's insolence, Valery revealed a whole new self to him, a thinking mechanism, an ability to register, to come to conclusions, to plan. She allowed her usually blank expression to focus on the situation, she listened for once not only to Crispin, but to Austin as well. She registered openly, in front of the servant, her disapproval, not of him, but of her husband. It might even have been her expression which egged Crispin on, and drove Austin to lose control, pushed him into firing him. It was almost as though the gardener were her spokesman. After he had gone Valery, indulging in her new habit of fidgetting plucked at a dandelion strewing it over the point of her shoe and kicking up little pieces of turf.

"Look Valery" he said, "the dandelions should be weeded. Crispin should do it."

She rooted one out, smirking. A milky fluid spread over her fingers.

"Let's go in" he said.

"You go in."

"Come upstairs with me."

"I have to tell Amy that Miss Lampton is coming to dinner tonight."

"There's no need to discuss what happened with Amy you know."

"I thought it was a joke."

"Crispin never jokes."

"But all he did was say 'Master' to you...I can't see anything so terrible about that?"

"He said 'Master Austin'. And for the first time too."

"He only called you that out of friendship. To remind you of your childhood."

"You won't come upstairs with me?"

"I must speak to Amy. I want things to go well. I want Miss Lampton to come over often."

"Why?"

"Don't you like her? I thought too she could help with the housekeeping. Give me advice, that sort of thing, neighborly hints." she said over her shoulder, scurrying into the house.

At least I fired him, he thought, knowing that Crispin would never leave. Why is he winning again? Why does she take his side? Whenever she's in the garden he's always around.

That morning she had been wandering listlessly around circling the lawn, Austin following her. When Crispin appeared she immediately perked up, asked him what flowers would come up in the summer, would there be poppies later on, geraniums, nasturtiums? "Put in nasturtiums" Austin said. "Certainly Mrs. Carver" Crispin bowed, and Austin suddenly said furiously, "Yesterday I heard a terrible caterwauling coming from your room. Get rid of it."

"You're m-m-mistaken."

"You won't get rid of it?"

"It's only a k-k-kitten."

"Get rid of it."

"Oh, but he can't, he musn't" Valery said.

"I can't. It's w-w-wounded."

"How full of pity..."

"I have a r-r-room..."

"In my house..."

"He does no harm" Valery said.

"And if n-n-no one else wants..."

"I will not listen to the caterwauling of the wounded..."

"You ever listen to yourself? Oh, s-s-sorry! Your will be done, Master Austin."

"Get out of my sight! Clear out. For good. At once." Austin screamed.

"He didn't mean anything." Valery said softly.

Austin who had overheard Amy in conversation with his wife wondered at the possibility of Valery's alliance with the servants. How could he even begin to guess how many complaints through the years they had been harboring against him. Probably Valery would arm herself secretly with the cook's gossip, for who knew if there did not exist behind that blank exterior a destructive force which he had only begun to experience? At most times she seemed an easy victim, ready to capitulate. It should have been simpler than disarming his father, whose manhood had so neatly been clipped, to force that fragile mind, and in the cleft to plant the seed of himself. And yet he knew that he would in some way have to make amends for what had happened today, would have to give Crispin some difficult task to reinstate him, to please Valery.

She shall have a balcony. Poised in the sky, illuminated by clouds she shall stand with her white arms on the balustrade. From her vantage point she shall observe my patience, her hair will cascade in my direction. The wings of her dress will fly upwards. Love me.

"A balcony?" she asked, the flicker of a smile. "Can Crispin really build a balcony?"

"I'll see to it."

Why did Crispin go about the almost impossible task of drilling into the stone facade of the house with an enthusiasm totally unbefitting a menial? Why did Valery take up her post beside him with such loyal regularity encouraging him as though the idea were his? Worst of all why did she have to spend so much time in the kitchen chattering with Amy about how the building was getting on, making it a private affair between the servants and herself? When it was miraculously completed she leaned out, way way out with shining eyes on Crispin as he bedded a clump of thyme, "It will s-s-smell nice" in the rock garden below, totally ignoring Austin.

"I must see about tonight's dinner. Miss Lampton is coming."

"Again?"

"I admire her terribly. I want to be just like her."

"That would be hard to manage." Impatience rising.

"I can try" she said.

"In that case why not start by wearing piles of makeup. I'm sick of your pale face. Do something about your disgusting pallor." His heart beat at the knowledge of how her fingers, tipped with rouge, would doodle ineptly about her cheeks until her face floating above him became a travesty. She hung out of reach on Crispin's platform.

"I never want to see you without lipstick again, do you hear? You ask your Miss Lampton for beauty advice."

He saw Crispin smiling as he planted bluebells and lilies in her rock garden, stuttering triumphantly as he reinstated himself in the household.

"Why not put color on your eyelids also, red maybe?"

Where was Crispin? Flattened against the trunk of the oak tree, hand to ear like a buffoon memorizing King Carver's words, tongue clicking in pity at the new Mrs. Carver's plight.

"Why can't you manage the household accounts?" he shouted at her.

"For God's sake stop crying. You're running mascara all over your face."

"I've asked you again and again to see to it that Amy doesn't serve such elaborate meals. They're sickening."

"Did you use my mother's book for a coaster?" he asked slapping her hand as she tried to hide it behind her back, noticing her little look of exultation as she ran sobbing from the room.

When her long day of mistakes was over she sat on the bed, in a lace nightgown with unironed bows all over the bodice, the sash heaped in her lap, her hair hanging in a tangled mess, one slipper teetering on her toes, the other in the middle of the floor, her clothes tossed beside her in an ungainly heap she knew would enrage him. He burst in the room to find her in all her private languor, like a little creature of the fields concentrating only on its own comfort.

"Behold the perfect wife." One night he rushed out of the room, "You make me sick. I'd rather sleep anywhere than beside you. I'd rather be in my old room than here."

And now everyone in the household knew that Valery spent suffocating nights under an ill fitting canopy which he had erected to commemorate the first year of his uneventful marriage. Kneeling by the single bed which step by clattering step he had dragged from the attic, he kept a mocking eye on Valery. On his orders, she stood by while he sowed the floor with nails.

"I think my dear, you will sleep nicely in this bed for it just fits you. You will sleep sweetly under this canopy." He was presenting her with an anniversary gift while she, empty handed, had not so much as blinked on being reminded what day it was.

"Never mind if it's too big, we must make do, don't you agree?" He was transported with glee on discovering that in order to put up the oversized framework it would have to be fixed to the floor: he set to work with the delirium of a celebrant at an orgy.

"I must put in some extra nails." and with each one he persuaded himself that he had passed his last sleepless night since what he was building was a coffin in which once he had closed the lid she would be incarcerated forever.

"Come and try it on'" Mutely she advanced towards him, hesitating by the bed.

"Go on."

"Why...what for...what...what do...you want?" she regarded him with that somnolence which he had never succeeded in piercing, pulling all the while on a hangnail and speaking in a faltering manner.

"Try it on for size."

"But what, what do you mean...where...it's much too low...can't you see that?" She appeared to be so confused that he was obliged to push her. The canopy was so low that landing in the material where she lolled momentarily as in a hammock she would have struck her head against the top had she been sitting upright. With an air of exaggerated affability he tugged at the cloth on which she sat and let it drop in front of her.

All he could see of Valery were her hands fidgeting with the tassels of the canopy fringe.

"Are you pleased with your new lodging?

"She's so pleased she doesn't answer," he whispered stagily. "I shan't disturb you in there, I assure you, no, I shall not disturb you."

"I see" she said. "Oh...yes, I do see..." Humbled and mortified would she ingratiate herself into his forgiveness, settle down in the vise of his arms? "I understand" she purred, and he could not miss her point. Her voice communicated quite distinctly neither her mortification nor her penitence, but her thanks.

GREEN

All my troubles started in the country. When I first saw my tongue reflected in a friend's parlor mirror, a piece of liver slashing between my teeth, the taste of it didn't revolt me and I excused the sounds it made for all the harm which had been done me.

It was all very well for him. He had his romance. Or if not he had the fantasy of it. The farmer's wife gave him a kiss at the Halloween party. Under the tables of manicotti and the tureens of ravioli they knelt, their foreheads touching. Her strong white arms and bare legs grew milky with the late hour and the whiskey drunk neat in an impulsive but monotonous manner. His tongue touched playfully the tip of her square nose. Her limbs stretched out like weeds in the fetid air under the cloth and soon their hairs were making a tangled mass on each other's shoulders, her bush of blonde and his briar of red. I burst out laughing and moved on.

We lived in a big square green high ceilinged room. An open staircase led to an unfinished attic. Splinters of sky gleamed through and the window panes didn't fit properly. The house had been built by the farmer's father for diversion, in his spare time between the clearing of mammoth oaks and elms and maples from the now smooth fields, of giant rooted rocks and even, it was told me, as we sat in the fitful warmth of pine wood, of skulls and arrowheads. The farmer's wife smiled slyly when I suggested we put a grate in front of the exploding fire. She said, It will only reduce the heat. I said, Are you cold then? She said, Not I.

Milo and the farmer's wife were the same height. Her body was lean and tough, a concentrated weight. Her eyes like small honed wedges slid into his soft and spilling flesh so swiftly he felt nothing but a cool void closing up behind her glance.

The story was that the farmer's father on groundhog day, too early in the spring to work the frozen earth, was yanking at the roots of a giant stump, he and his horse haltered shoulder to shoulder. Suddenly the farmer leapt strangle-eyed from his traces. His chest arched against the rope. His crimson face seemed trying to rise into the sky, his hands shot up, and out of his distended throat came strange gutturals. Then the horse began to whinny and thrash from side to side until the rope cut into the foaming hide. An icy rain started up and the horse slipped in the mixture of snow and ooze around the roots, and the man slid down on its neck. Only the horse's eye moved in a frenzied circle. So they buried the horse and the man in the hole they had dug and for tombstone they replanted the stump above them. And it's still there, festooned now with young shoots and small leaves.

Milo took to staring out the rattling windows. No matter how loud I talked his backbone gave no sign of hearing. His eyes were large, very brown, spongey, dangerously tender. The countryside oozed into his long patient ogling as into a marsh. I stood my ground on the side of the road that separated our house from theirs and laughed. I said, Who would have dreamed you'd come to this?

One day Milo and I were sleeping back to back with handkerchiefs over our eyes and hands over our ears when we were awakened by the cow in labor. Milo jumped out of bed and said he must go see. I said such things are better imagined than seen. Stay then, he said, and I hurried after him the short distance between our house and their barn. Half his size and in my fluffy rabbit robe I tripped along imagining I was a little child about to learn the facts of life, so trusting so innocent I placed my wee fingers in his big red paw and felt with awe the ticking of his venus' mound. His expression livened immediately he saw her, standing in the muck and dung, dressed in narrow jeans and leather knee boots and a tight red jersy, cheeks aglow with the joy, she said, of new life. Her tall blond indistinguishable twin sons stood stiffly by as she hallooed her biceps toward Milo. He made a gesture of kissing her hand, though of course I saw very well under her courtly bow how his warm gaze dug into the unsubtle outline of her vigorous groin and how her bluebottle eyes answered in kind. I looked straight at the boys and giggled. We entered the milking shed. The monstrous bulk of the cow was penned in a space so small every time she moved the planks thundered. I shouted, Can't you give her more room for Christ's sake? Alan Alan grasped my arm painfully but, jarred by my voice she was already trying to turn over and rise to her knees. He put his hand between her eyes and with his index finger scratched softly under her sawed off horns until she looked back at him with huge sucking eyes. Behind me pressed Margie and Milo. I felt their teeth on the back of my neck. In the airless shed there was no sound except for the buzzing of gigantic flies. I burst out laughing. At that the cow gave another startled heave and managed to turn over, braying all the while as though in some new unimaginable agony. Margie looked angrily at Milo. Milo looked up at the rafters but it was Alan Alan, his eyes grown violet with tenderness for his beast, who looked at me one harsh second through pale nordic lashes, a glint of malice, a foreboding of bad times to come. I would have been on my way then and there but at the narrow entrance the twins stood with identical expressions. Then Alan plunged both arms down into the pen where her brown hide clotted with foam and mud seethed and suddenly her swollen sides stiffened and she threw her head back on her round moist neck and Alan Alan leapt into the pen, squatted down beside her, and encouraged her with murmurs and love talk, and behind me I felt Milo's tongue nestling to the music in Margie's cheek as the beauteous bubble of placenta oozed out from under the rigid tail.

Another day Margie and Milo played on the green rug of our green walled house. The ceiling too was green. Everything was green, the long hard sofa, the two matching chairs, the mantel piece, the staircase going up to an open hole, so that it was hard to tell the difference between the furniture and the room. The sky was full of more snow about to fall. A lull in the weather flickered through the window and she, her arms glued to her sides, rolled from one end of the room to the other. From his haunches he watched scrupulously. I too had difficulty keeping pace with her blurred features. She was drowning down there, an expressionless eye shot by, pale lips rose to the surface stifled by her hair. I jumped down from the sofa and stood in the center of the room. The toe of my leather shoe hooked into her side. Face down she gave a startled cry and whipped around, her back up my ankle. It took her a second to realize what was going on. Thus we stared at each other, her blue of ice, my brown of mud, till Milo came between us.

Margie Alan was running naked through the light snow, her face turned up to the sky. The icy branches of the apple trees whipped against her body. Milo's breath covered the window pane in fuzzy rivulets. A band of white encircled her top and another her bottom. Above, between, and below was the familiar flesh we had watched simmering all summer, laid out solemnly an hour a day between reflectors, and swathed in a flowered bikini, gift of her husband, she said. Snow settled on her shoulders and hair. Is she insane? I asked. Milo mumbled, Hush. Among the apple trees was a slender pear tree. Many times I heard her say with a kind of gloating pride, that tree in the spring looks like a bride, while Alan Alan watched her lips dreamily. Was he watching her now, taking a little time off from his endless chores? Suddenly she embraced the tree. I started to laugh and couldn't stop. In the window pane Milo's eyes switched from awe to fury and blank amazement. I looked out, still hiccupping. With a leap from the balls of her feet she swung from the tree's first branch and then with the phenomenal strength hidden in her pearly biceps snapped the wood neatly at the trunk. Then I saw her eyes jerk sidewise at our house, a thin blue intentional glint that pierced the heavy air and moist window and Milo's round brown bovine stare. His hands itched against the glass. My hiccups came back full force. Margie Alan dragging the pear branch ran lightly like a nymph from our curiosity, through the long alley of trees calling Alan, Alan, Alan. The barn door opened across the snowy mute fields. The pear branch in Alan Alan's huge arm circled the farm buildings, and came up with a swoosh on her waiting behind. And all along the switch as though it were spring bloomed a thick profusion of perfectly shaped and artful giggles.

She sprang off my foot, agile as a circus. She said, It's all a matter of keeping fit in the winter as well as in the summer. Winters I take hot baths followed by a tumble in the snow. Her hard fingers on my shoulders kept me there at attention. I put my palms on hers. We were two sisters. I said, Are you crazy? Milo's head tried to push itself between our entwined arms. Watch, she said, what I can do. Then she squatted down and slowly, at first quivering and gradually steadying, raised herself on her hands and up went her hard ripe bottom, her knees and calves like a tail behind suddenly swished to the right and then to the left. I said, later he beats you with birch bark, right? Still upside down, through her hair, she said, It's all a matter of keeping one's body tingling throughout the year. The nape of her neck was surrounded by tendrils of moist weeds. I laughed some more and went out into the heavy afternoon.

Alan Alan was deaf. I didn't know that until the day I tried to share a secret with him. I thought he was blushing at my words but it was simply his apprehension at having me so close

34

to him. Or perhaps he caught in my expression something con-
spiratorial, something hushed. We were sitting in the kitchen.
He was drinking his mid morning coffee. He kept his face in the
mug the whole time sipping so slowly his throat hardly worked.
His eyes through the steam gave an appearance of mildness. I
felt somewhat encouraged. I said, slapping him on the back in a
pally manner, Alan, Alan Alan is certainly an amusing name. He
drew back. It was very hot in the kitchen. The sound of the
stove hissing took my breath away. The small curtained windows were covered with vapor for it was zero weather and the
cows' tongues steamed at the salt licks in the hardening
meadow. Finally he put his cup down. There was a plate of
anise cookies on the table. He drew it towards him and chose
himself one. The scent of anise seed stuck between his teeth
filled the airless room. I felt the dizziness preceding a plunge
and suddenly grasped his hand midway to his mouth and keeping my attention away from his flaming face and my burning
throat whispered pell mell my message into his furry ear. I let
go his wrist and set back exhausted. He moved another pace
away from me. He stuck his index finger into his ear and
scratched. Then he shook his head as if his ear were filled with
spit.

I was imagining all the while how that heavy set hard fingered
man would in three strides reach the crest of the hill, how her
cheek would thud against the rocks between whose slimy sides
the stream barely ran. For all water there is shallow, the ponds, the
lakes, the rivers all covered with sediment. Milo lost a moccasin
running after her through the slimy frog bed, in such a hurry he
rushed on barefoot. And what did it matter to him if he lost a
toe or two in the inclement weather he wasn't used to? She was
naked. Sitting in a tree, her legs wide open, her head dangling
between on her long spine, her hair swinging. He kept his shirt
on but he took his pants off. She lowered herself on to his
penis. Goose pimpled and blue tipped it stretched bravely and
even trustingly into the freezing forest.

She had strangely long nails for a farmer's wife, varnished to
a point. Milo caught her wrist. His red hand against her blue
vein sank from sight. Cows stood around them. I guffawed. I
called, Milo, come back to bed. I saw a strand of her hair
meshed between the swinging udders. He took a step towards
her. The cows' legs were firm as the sides of a pen. Their ears
flicked against him below their blunted horns. Imperceptibly
they shifted ranks. He could hardly breathe now so tenderly

their haunches pressed against him. I opened my mouth to laugh but before the sound came out she pressed her muzzle into his face. Her eyes were huge swamps. She flicked her tail indifferently.

MY BROWN FRIEND

SIMON VESTDIJK

Translation from the Dutch by

M. C. Duyvendak

Although I must have played there from early childhood, I have almost no recollection of the close surroundings of my home. The house itself, a bulging forehead above the snaggle teeth of a little shop, is streaked with cracks; the facade seems to be split by adversity, which actually we never knew. Discrepancies were everywhere. Instead of the rooms simply opening into each other they are set (as I think of them) askew within each other, as if they had to serve as each other's cupboard-beds. Memories of children's games are halted by awful door sills; the beds on the contrary are small, shrunken, as if burned out. In the evening a pear-shaped brass lamp shiny with petroleum (as a child I used to speak of 'Petera' with a throaty 'r' imitated by my older sister. 'Petera' was for me both petroleum and associated with snakes, but perhaps also with petermen, stinging fish of which I always suspected there would be one or more in the green parchment-covered jars boys brought home after a long afternoon of fishing, along the ditches surrounding the town), shed a strong sharp light on the bald head of my prematurely old, but naturally cheerful father, who at that hour usually sat in a cloud of smoke behind his account books, stamping with impatience when they did not balance, which made the sailing ship in the glass bell on top of the clothes press rattle in sympathy, as if it were suddenly full of pennies and was offering the missing one to my father. In my memory my mother is beautiful and dark, but resignedly lower middle class and also aged before her time, and even my sister seemed to be struggling against the approaching weight of years. She would passionately sing long songs in the kitchen, on the stairs, in her room on summer evenings when other girls fall silent. She was always excited and on the go, always on the point of doing something important and decisive, of taking a vital step. With fiery red cheeks and flashing black eyes, she dashed back and forth to the neighbours' to make plans for evening parties. Although she was only just nineteen at the time my story begins, she wanted to be the life and soul of everything; she felt her youth not so much as a natural handicap, but rather as an extra spur; and there was that common family trait: feeling slighted, imagining we were despised by the town and just for that reason wanting to vie with the flower of its notables. However prosperous and respected a citizen, my father naturally could not expect jonkheer so and so with his Irish setter to bow to my mother on the street. He understood, and my mother understood, although it was a thorn in the flesh. Nevertheless, my sister celebrated her nineteenth birthday with a fit of temper, because that setter accompanied by a non-bowing jonkheer had passed her. She instilled manners, and she had me take messages to the parson, Mr. Kalmans, about the little church choir that depended on her clear soprano, and dealt me cuffs under the table if I teased her about boys or young men too base in her eyes to relieve her from the obsession of the jonkheer. All the same I was fond of her. Her face charmed me, and I still believe she was at all events too beautiful for that little town. She was not vain in the ordinary sense, nor was her head turned, she was frank and honest, only she did expect the world to give her what she was not willing to work for. Her purposely dressing less well than other girls was more an instinctive gesture than a sign of false humility. In this respect the only duplicity in which I sometimes caught her was her complete lack of interest in my classical studies. But higher education at that time was not yet part of a girl's training, and I can hardly believe she was jealous of my natural privilege and showed it in this way.

All the rest of the town for me is built around the classical school which formed as it were its citadel. A mighty arm of the sea — mighty in imagination — that created and destroyed horizons, gave birth almost volcanically to islands out of fogs and submerged them again like sand bars in a spring tide, made the little town something so temporary and transient that the big gleaming building with its systematic knowledge and its, for the most part, very energetic teachers was decidedly needed to give credence to a permanent settlement of people with a clearly defined purpose in life. Nature pressed the city flat, dispersed it into back streets, paused in fright before the old-time town hall but denied it behind its back in a particularly filthy cattle market, whence it escaped along brown gutters, towards the one shopping street with that peculiar fusty, stifling, vaguely sensuous odour of yard goods, which in as many as four Jewish stores (my father did not know these people although himself chiefly a dry goods merchant) was reefed between thumb and forefinger along a yard stick — and for the rest kept to the really handsome, shady city walls much too good for the dilapidated junk inside. In front of the recently-built country house of the nonbowing jonkheer (he lived there with an older sister who was known as 'Lady Sticks'; not satisfied with this misnomer we called her at school 'Lady Acheron', secretly shivering at her appearance; she was tall and muscular with dull eyes and skin like grated candles) nature once more spread herself obligingly in a delightful garden, but that really was all, and she promptly struck out vindictively with views of improbably lush green cattle-filled meadows, low dunes, mounds of old irons and rubbish, crooked windmills, bleached bones of Sea Beggars, towards a horribly bare sea, foggy, panting, wide as a thousand canals flowing by the basalt piers to withdraw into a little muddy harbour, meeting place for Calvinist sailors weakened by inbreeding, and then, with a few turns streaming back into itself without breakers, without horizon, with scarcely a fishing boat, but only a lot of crabs walking sideways on the dike, pervading everything with an indescribable stench of rotting jelly-fish and winkles, which in spite of its origin was in its effect on our spirits very like the smell of unbleached muslin in the main street through which as boys, after playing an afternoon on the beach, we walked in little groups, tired and sandy and a little fearful because once more everything had seemed so endless and all in vain.

An old city gate with some sort of coat of arms on it closed off the grey wide square like a prolongation of the shopping street. Old fishermen leaned against it and spat across dreadfully yellow butchers' dogs. Yes, and here the sea we thought we had escaped began again. It was everywhere. The sea (or fog) was visible on three sides of the town. Whoever heard of such a thing? The only difference was that at the gate it smelled of dried dabs instead of rotting jelly-fish and that suddenly, God knows from where, like a brand new world out of the murky chaos, there sprang up a little lighthouse just around the corner from the gate, striped black and yellow like a zebra, long-necked like a giraffe and waving a light at night, of course. In just what rhythm that light went back and forth I did not know for a long time. I always thought it was not visible from the land anyway, or even from the sea close in, but that you would have to go far, far out on the cursed element to catch sight of it like a diplomatic wink intended for the other side of the conference table. Perhaps even as far as the Gravel Bar, which was submerged at high tide and where older boys sometimes rowed to hunt for shells. But even the Gravel Bar was a foggy idea for me; sometimes it was there and sometimes not; something that meant danger and yet was only made of sand. No need to say after all this how I hated the sea. I hated the sea because it was forever trying to be different. I hated it because of its famous past, exhaled by dead winkles, because of its inert passion, its nervous multiform cumbrousness, and its inhospitality in always casting the little boats we made ourselves back on to the dike. If the classical school had not been there, I would have despaired, but as it was there I got along until my fifteenth or sixteenth year.

And so existence, conscious and verifiable, began for me with my entrance examination, an event that projected its bright rays for years ahead. Happy time in which things are discovered! Probably the feeling of happiness is no greater at that age than later, but a boy is more active, supple, quick, open, and an adult confuses this with happiness and gaiety. I can remember young colts who were melancholics at heart. My friend Gerard Steierman was so far an exception in that he combined calm and dignified behaviour with a very cheerful temperament, but still of a special kind and decidedly not youthful in its imperturbability. With his childishly surprised eyes, his lilting and precise Overijsel accent — all the words ending in 'en' were bitten off — he seemed an innocent; we were slow finding out that he was a philosopher and an unexpectedly sensible fellow. But even if he always stayed at the head of the class without much trouble, his sceptical philosophical disposition made him something quite different from a teacher's pet. I lost sight of him later. He probably became a surveyor as he always said he would; he was too modest to go to the University; actually, it was still an exception to be allowed to study. When the other boys noticed that their teasing and mimicking his Overijsel speech could not change the expression of those grey-blue orbs, he immediately became popular, although on the playing-field — we played chiefly tip-cat — he, unlike myself, could not keep up. But outside of sports and homework there was still a third world for him.

He was very mysterious at first about the atom theory he had thought out; it cost me three long evening walks before I heard him say in a choking voice, "An atom is a whirl in the ether", moved for the first time, for the first time solemn. Or rather he had always been solemn and I had felt this coming. Months followed when we philosophized seriously, first about matter, then about mind, then about both and then about girls; but that did not last long for Gerard was so deeply shocked by the things I confided to him, although I found his confidences much worse, that he did not say anything for days and just stared and stared, attentive and cheerful, at notions in the air and still without the least anger. All the same, a slight estrangement entered into our relations and after that we only philosophized in Bible class, that is, under direction. How I wished I could hear more about those atoms. It seems to me a theory worthy of being hatched in the foggy place where we belonged. Active and omnipresent as they were, in the sea water, between the basalt blocks, in the old fishermen's tobacco juice, those mysterious whirling particles compensated for the town's monotony almost as much as a haunted house: but I never could get anything more definite from Jard (that is what we called him in Zeeland), and perhaps he had already forgotten the whole theory.

I regarded all the teachers as young, bouncing fellows, bursting with animal spirits and facts they wished to impart to us. Even the Head cannot have been older than forty. Disorder was unknown. There were whispers about a model school, iron discipline maintained with playful ease. It was true that strange figures sometimes appeared among the pupils of the higher classes: boys who could not keep up at other schools or who had been expelled for worse reasons. We had them from all parts of the country. Each year the first day of school it looked as though we were getting some new teachers in those surly pipe-smoking strangers, who did not fit into the benches of the third class and who had the sea in their heads, or pubs or girls. Because the newcomers, in spite of their tricks, were remarkably well disciplined, just like colonists or real convicts, the school did not suffer much from its fate as a deportation colony. The outsiders were greatly esteemed by us younger boys although they took absolutely no notice of us; their heroic deeds were recounted, exaggerated and later even attributed to others, who had nothing whatever to do with them; but for actual epidemic wickedness that might have been feared, there was too much Zeeland peasant blood in our classes; diligent rather narrow-minded roundheads, nice boys mostly, not brilliant, not demoniac, good Dutchmen with a drop of Spanish blood as they say, blood used to controlling itself and being controlled. Except for the teasing Gerard Steierman had to endure for a while, I never noticed any unpleasant spirit among the native pupils; even the Jews were spared. And it goes without saying that the slights complained of by my parents which, real or imagined, left such a deep mark on my sister's character, made not the slightest impression on me.

This story really begins in the late summer between my second and third school years. It was preceded by a carefree, long vacation with plenty of fresh air, many talks with Gerard Steierman and a few love affairs such as boys have, not going deep and entirely a part of my general emotional state of unreasoned elation. I was perfectly rested and very open to new impressions. It was the week before school was to open when I and Gerard and a few other boys were walking back and forth in front of the school building, impatient perhaps. The sea, the fields, the ditches, had no more attraction for us, we were bored with rowing, pole jumping and fishing; to be honest, we longed for books and a teacher's voice over our heads. Even if we did curse the school, naturally, it was with secret love. We discussed the possibilities of the penal colony; what guests would we lodge? "Look, there," Gerard's finger pointed towards the row of buildings next to the school. We all of us idly gazed in that direction and at first noticed nothing but some fourth class boys standing in a group smoking. Four figures separated themselves from the others and sauntered towards us; I had no feeling that this meant anything. For that matter I recognized three of the four, two being last year's outsiders — Jelte Veenstra, a boy from the north who had struck a teacher with brass knuckles, looking like a sombre John Bull with lubberly alcoholic's eyes, and the impudent slender curly-headed Charles Desmet, about whom there were whispers of pilfering, and finally, the son of one of the yard goods Jews in our shopping street, generally called Rusman, though I believe his name was Heiman Asser Polak. This Rusman, squarely built but supple in his movements and strikingly dark in appearance — the reason for his nickname which we meant to be flattering — had acted for several years as a guide for a succession of new exiles and was able to be so obliging because his deliberate laziness kept him in the fourth class. I had long been rejoicing at the prospect of becoming his classmate. He commanded our respect by a certain silent reserve quite different from the usual notion "Jew" which always unintentionally suggests something noisy. Moreover, Rusman really had a handsome face. I can still remember, at about the age of twelve, standing watching a game of tip-cat when a man behind me, a kind of boatman with rings in his ears and a grey beard stained with tobacco juice around his loose gaping mouth, said to another, "There's a good-looking boy!" Although there were five or six boys playing, I knew at once whom he meant. It was the first time I heard one male praise another for his physical beauty, and for some reason that insignificant incident was firmly fixed in my mind, though I do not believe I may be suspected of anything but pleasure in having a real grown-up confirm the admiration we felt for a schoolmate.

Because all these three boys had a perfectly everyday significance for me, I was hardly prepared to find something among them that easily predominated, and according to entirely different standards than the ones they represented. The group sauntered past us at a distance of about six yards with that fourth one in their midst who was lame: that was the first thing I noticed about him. I thought: a lame boy, what is he doing with Rusman and with Desmet and Jelte Veenstra? At that moment I received a look full of scorn sent out above that miserable lurch that thrust him forward. It was impossible the newcomer could have guessed my thoughts. I was nevertheless struck by the cold self-control evident in his whole being, the symmetry of his slender body that seemed to bear its affliction with proud stoicism like an eternally imposed gymnastic exercise, the lines of rebellion, injury and disdain around the sharply drawn mouth. What did it all mean? When the bitter sight of the cripple, who was no longer paying any attention to me, had gone by, emotion rose like a lump in my throat. Why should that boy notice me? I could still see the pale contemptuous face, slightly ruddy, with rare summer freckles, the nose delicate, short and blunt, the pouches under the brown, cold, scornfully searching eyes — and at last I saw nothing except that hunting and groping look in a face I could not recall. There is something coppery about that boy, I thought. There he was, sauntering in the distance, limping, his short brown coat flapping in the wind, and yet in my eyes so inimitably distinguished that it seemed as if an exiled prince surrounded by common followers — two squires and a dragoman — had left me the riddle of his taunting revolt. But why was that scorn directed at me who knew I was as good as anybody in the world? It is true I am small and rather ugly; but I am well built and fairly strong and I do not believe the transition period was the most disadvantageous for me as it often is for boys. In spite of my aversion for the sea I excelled in fishing and swimming; this very summer I had rowed to the Gravel Bar three times. I was not stupid either, even Gerard Steierman, though he sometimes called me a fool, looked up to me. While recalling that indifferent procession I puzzled and puzzled and then I suddenly thought that Rusman, who knew everything about every boy, might have said something about me just before that look was aimed at me. All day I kept on puzzling in vague fear, in dark enchantment. Gerard and the others did not even know his name.

Three days later we were lingering by one of our ditches just outside the town. Gerard Steierman, I and the two Evertsen brothers: Henk, a great big easy-going fellow and Boudewijn, a little younger, much smaller and rather ill-natured. Gerard was just trying a take-off with our only pole held out in front of him, when I noticed at the other end of the field across the ditch the same threateningly indifferent little group we had seen three days ago. They approached, swinging their arms, their legs apart like sailors on deck, the limper in their midst with his loose coat flapping around him in that strange, almost birdlike way. My heart beat fast. But Gerard too seemed to have sensed some sort of mysterious danger; he slowed up, came to a standstill on the edge of the ditch and began to jab in the water with the pole, as if he wanted to kill some monsters of the deep before risking the jump. Just as he turned around, a stone whizzed by between Henk Evertsen and me: the dancing arms of the limper had taken aim; nothing had changed in his listless, sauntering, uneven gait; the faint, disdainful smile showed in his coppery face, and then there came another stone in our direction that plunked into the water, and still another almost striking Gerard Steierman's right arm. "Quit that!" shouted Henk Evertsen in a calm voice. But I thought: 'Don't shout, that stone wasn't meant for you. It's a present from that boy to me.' For I had seen it, that this throwing motion, without the least effort or design, almost like part of the limping rite, expressed the same contempt; it was the gesture of driving away a dog, or of a French marquis of the Old Regime throwing mouldy bread to the canaille. I never once noticed him picking up those stones; probably his companions handed them to him un-noticed. "Go ahead, Jard!" said Henk Evertsen sharply and still more calmly. The besiegers had halted, but it really was ridiculous to think of them as besiegers, that simply never happened with us; it was not that kind of school. With his round eyes blinking at the sky, Gerard also seemed to be busy summing up this experience, the result being a theoretical assurance of perfect safety on the other side of the ditch. Nevertheless, he retired somewhat for a longer take-off, so that we all three expected to see him swerve at the last minute. A shout arose from the four when he jogged into motion: the boy with the brown face limped forward, nearly to the mud bank that separated the ditch from the higher meadow, slipped on the edge and stood still. The idea was for the jumper to land on the higher ground. "Go ahead, Jard!" Gerard Steierman, who had actually turned back a second time, nodded reassuringly as if he were now quite sure how this ditch had to be taken. In the meantime I had a clear view of the lame boy's face; it seemed to be an open book for me, although he was not looking in my direction. His dark brown eyes were narrowed in thought. There was the provoking smile in the corners of his mouth, but the whole face, tilted back expectantly, had something so frail and feminine that the peculiar ruddy glow that covered it could hardly be attributed to anything but shame. His feet stood almost entirely in the water. The other three who remained at a distance yelled in turn "Who's next?" and Henk Evertsen kept shouting back, "Will you quit it? What have we done to you?" rather senselessly, because no more stones were being thrown, and the lame boy stood there as if he were going to catch minnows with his bare hands. To the sound of great cheers, Gerard, red in the face from Henk's alternating urging and shouting, started the long take-off for the third time. The pole shot into the water at a slant and seemed to sink deeper into the mud than usual — too deep. With legs spread, Gerard hovered over against the steep refractory slope, but he had passed dead centre and his own weight would carry him if not to the edge of the meadow then at least on to the mud a few yards from the stranger. The latter suddenly gave a leap, bent over, stretched his right arm straight out and caught the pole in the spare between Gerard's two hands. At first the arm bent far back, then, jerking and shoving, it was stuck out like a ramrod. The fist, gripping so hard the color left it, held the pole so motionless at an angle of forty-five degrees that the jumper could do nothing but slide down slowly into the slimy water. That was something for a philosopher. He squirmed back and forth like a monkey! I could no longer see the face of his attacker very well, but I'm certain that taunting expression never left it for a second and that peculiar feminine, expectant, sleepy look and that glow of shame. Luckily everything turned out better than could be expected. What we now got to see was a feat. On the point of sinking in the water, Gerard was seized by two strong hands and with one heave set down on the driest part of the muddy bank; the pole stood trembling, then leaned over to the left. All this was carried out so quickly and skilfully that we could not resist the impulse to join in the applause from the opposite side. Only Henk Evertsen swore under his breath and stuck one leg out, as if he wanted to spring over the ditch to go to the help of the victim. But not the slightest harm was done to Gerard. Without a spot on his clothes, he could scramble on to the meadow where the other, after rubbing his hands together, had already preceded him. And there he went hobbling off, accompanied by the others, without looking around, a strange brown insect in a flapping jacket. Desmet and Veenstra did still shout mocking words in our direction; but their leader seemed not to want to spoil the effect of his performance, and they were already too far away for us to understand them. Or had Boudewijn Evertsen caught some of their words? As we walked slowly home, with the pole that had not been hard to recover like a very nearly dishonored trophy between us, talking it over, he suddenly said to me, 'Did you hear what they called out about your sister?' I shook my head and saw his brother punch him to keep him quiet. Completely absorbed in the spectacle beside the ditch, I thought no more about it; the well-known boys' habit of ignoring sisters in public was still entirely mine; moreover, I knew Boudewijn was not averse to malicious inventions. School began three days later.

The first weeks after this I was so much under the influence of Hugo Verwey — that was his name — that I scarcely noticed whatever else went on around me. It was said that he was the son of a high-ranking officer and must already be all of eighteen. Nobody knew where he came from; the reason for his deportation, however, could not remain a secret. Drink, women, theft, those were the three cardinal sins which along with the usual street and school misdemeanours regularly recurred among our clients and in this case it was 'women' — girls, maids. But how? Well, I need not repeat all that gossip here, suffice it that in the midst of his comrades' most scabrous bragging, never an indecent word, I was repeatedly assured, crossed his lips, and this perhaps proves more than a whole list of closet sins. Those who are obsessed by women do not talk about women. Indeed, at Hugo Verwey's age all this is not so much the result of

48

unsatisfied sensuality that must manifest itself, at any cost, be it only in words, as it is of an urge to action, courage and enterprise and there was convincing evidence that he had these.

Our gymnastic teacher, an old sergeant with a moustache, would have gone through fire and water for him and truly not because his father was his former commander, because the man did not care a hoot for that. It was rather the stunt he performed in the gymnasium, including the double giant swing to which his affliction added a very special glory. He naturally dropped out when anything depended on the use of his one defective group of muscles: he excelled in rowing, but he could hardly swim. Our sergeant called him "a brave sportsman with his arms, hot stuff, young sirs!" He said this in a voice hoarse with emotion. Moreover, if this is not sufficiently impressive, there was the school: his behaviour in the fourth class could be admired at second hand by the lower classes. As far as I was able to find out, he made a speciality of teaching our teachers manners — our young, lively, good-tempered teachers. The following went the rounds as a good joke. Mr. Ramacher, a short, fat little man who gaily and carelessly taught Dutch grammar, had the habit of sitting on the table before the class with his legs crossed. Probably because he thought of himself as a writer, he wore his hair long. His having small, inexpressive, unobservant eyes still does not explain how Hugo Verwey, who sat on the front bench at his feet could with impunity pick one of those long blond hairs from his thigh with his thumb and forefinger and with a disgusted expression drop it on the floor. No, the teacher had certainly seen it, but he was afraid of his groomer. That was our explanation, and I still believe it was the right one.

I must, however, add here that this proof of cool affrontery scarcely made any impression on me at that time. I was satiated with Hugo Verwey himself, with his image. It was not for what he did, but for what he was that I used to dream of him. It would even have been more satisfactory to me if he had not attracted so much public attention: this way he was not mine alone! He never took any more notice of me when he limped up and down in front of the school in his brown jacket, surrounded by his little court whose swaying bodies seemed to express their aversion to the repulsive chore imposed on this young prince as much as their hawking and spitting and vomiting curses, which no one ever heard him do. In fact, he spoke so little I don't even remember the sound of his voice in those early days. I never

49

again gazed into those coldly observant, dark-ringed eyes. But the more unapproachable he seemed, the more he filled my mind. There was an alluring terror in the evocation of that freckle-spotted face that once had been turned towards me like a challenge, a command, a condemnation. I pondered strenuously, as if my thoughts must bore through that strange arrogant blushing mask. Who was he? What had that boy been through? How did he feel? What did he mean? His eyes pursued me, insolent, searching, defensive, accusing, concealing and at the same time revealing. Each encounter was a fresh surprise, an oppressive festal occasion, something that could only happen once, and yet it was repeated. I yielded to queer day dreams, in which I met Hugo Verwey alone, beside the sea, and walked and talked with him as I did with Gerard Steierman, no others along, no followers. Because I realized vaguely that then the newcomer would be quite different, that he might well tell me what had driven him to this little town, and why his look was so sullen and mocking, so severe and yet so listless, and why he despised me. I thought he had despised me, because then naturally there would be no sign of scorn. A friend! Yes, for the first time I longed for something of the kind. Gerard the philosopher had really always been more of a pastime, a superficial game of wits to which anyone can lend himself. This exceptional Hugo Verwey, however, was intended for me alone, though he might be two or three years older than I. I never strove for a clearer understanding of this feeling, but I know now, I know it as if it were written in a book; it was love; it was precisely the same that is felt for women, only without sensuality. The lack of judgment characteristic of the Eros at that age, I experienced it bodily — no, not bodily, mentally.

This ardent desire to lay everything at his feet, to make myself his slave for eternity, winged my thoughts to bolder heights than atom theories. The image of Hugo Verwey endowed my life with a broadness only belied in appearance by the smarting, lancinating sharpness which marked that image. It was as if a sharp needle injected a narcotic fluid, blurring everything. When I beheld him I had a very definite sensation in my head of prickling or mild pain, strictly localized either on the left or right side. But when I thought of him in solitude, all was spacious and happy, with the indescribable nervous tingling felt when about to undertake a journey or anticipating a great transformation in one's life.

The fact that I was not ashamed and only concealed my condition in order not to have to bother anybody with riddles proves my complete lack of awareness of the abyss this infatuation hid. I could not have explained it, but the possibility of being in love never occurred to me. If anyone had given me an exact description of what I felt, I should have been grateful, even if it meant he knew everything. After about a month I suddenly imagined my sister knew because she acted so gay; but I thought perhaps my gaiety had infected her, and I was not a little surprised when she said: 'How solemn you look.' For half a day I was widly exuberant without, however, being able to compete with her. She sang as if the walls must burst; she ran around constantly with urgent communications that did not yet exist or still had to be formulated; her activity was only equalled by her fury if anyone doubted its reason. Its origin was the soprano part she had for the first time to sing in the Christmas cantata, a capricious piece by the singing teacher Balkom, consisting of psalm texts set to his own music. Did she not at last equal the Reverend Kalmans himself in her devoutness and, in the weight of her formal admonitions, Lady Sticks, the president of the little Protestant church choir? That is what she thought (later I knew that even this was not so; she was only a reflection of our teasing that moulded from without the suggestible nineteen-year-old); but when she burst into the living-room, feverish with animation, she looked more like a maenad with her hair pinned up, and my brother had to raise her hand and my father looked at the sail boat that rattled in its glass bell like an oracle speaking djinn of the thousand and one nights in his bottle. And even if I did not see much of her because all I saw was that other one, her deep red cheeks and moist, glittering eyes sometimes pierced through my preoccupation, and what else could I do but complete the triumphantly resounding line: "He that is Our God is the God of salvation" by bleating "And Sophie is bursting with elation", whereupon she chased me through the whole house until the shop girl came upstairs to say the clients were afraid to stay in the shop because another bolt of twill had fallen down.

She surprised me most when once on a long October evening, she started to talk about my school. That had never happened before. We were sitting together at the living-room table, I with my home-work. She stretched out her open hand and said, mocking: "You'll be awfully learned, Henk. Professor Mannoury!" "Doesn't that sound good? Oh, but Gerard knows a lot more; he thinks up things about science, about atoms! We hadn't even had that subject in class."

"Wouldn't you rather be an officer?"

"An officer?"

"Then you can travel back and forth to Breda. Or couldn't you? Or a naval officer? Oh! no, you hate the sea, the sea hates you —" gay and excited she burst out laughing in her usual way, then she flung her arms out wide so that the material of one of our finest silk blouses spanned her bosom (she had never worn silk before, I suddenly realized, and thought of the cantata), took a deep breath and seemed to be listening. I heard a step in the shop, a few words exchanged with the sales girl, who was free that evening and on the point of leaving, and then the same step on the stairs. "There's Mother!" shouted Sophie. Carolling, she dashed for the door and disappeared. A little later I heard her voice in the kitchen alternating with my mother's soothing tones. In the growing twilight that turned my paper blue against the dark background of the worn plush tablecloth, where a few crumbs always stuck, I continued to work. The tobacco smell of my father's snorting pipe was something stagnant, something dead, but the sail boat rolled gently and insistently on top of the clothes press, riding on the waves that rose from the kitchen. Sophie's unfortunate reference would not leave my mind, and more than ever I felt conscious of the sea surrounding everything. Perhaps I really was afraid of the sea; if I were not such a good rower and swimmer, I might really be destined to drown or at least to taste of death by drowning like that fisherman on the Gravel Bar when the tide came in, who pulled his boots off under water just when he began to see lovely flowers and himself as a small boy. There she came stumbling up the stairs again; the door was flung wide open and a clarion call scattered my dreams.

"Cakes, cakes, Henk!"

"What's that you say?"

"Cakes! Next week! You mustn't eat any lunch."

I only found out the following day that the next rehearsal of the choir was to be held at our house. They were not wealthy enough always to hire a hall and our front room was large and high. As she was not only the president, but actually one of the altos, even Lady Sticks was coming. Important guests these. Various alterations were made in all our costumes; for me my first long trousers because it might very well happen that someone or other would run into me, though for the rest my participation was to be only in the cakes. I understood vaguely that Sophie, instead of letting me know everything at once, which would have exposed her to my mockery, had first wanted to express her enthusiasm in another way and her subsequent behaviour confirmed this idea. Mr. Balkom and Lady Acheron were the trumps she held over me; nothing more was said about the officer or the naval officer. In that spick and span front room I can still see our chairs and a few more borrowed ones arranged in three rows, I see the glasses, the piles of cakes on the sideboard, and the nods my sister gave from me to those piles and then again towards her mother about whom at this critical moment she was much more concerned than usual. My father sat smoking his cigar in his shirt-sleeves in order to save his best jacket. In reality it was not likely that any one of us would be shown to the guests, unless the house caught fire. In the evening dress she wore, Sophie looked beautiful to me and very refined and above all, happy. Was not all the shame caused her by not knowing notables going to be effaced? I still see the white cloth she threw over her head when she did the last dusting; I still smell the odour of the little sausages in the kitchen, I hear the sail boat sounding the alarm at every hasty step until my father took it up and set it on the floor, which revealed for the first time how old and dusty it had got under its glass bell. And then I hear the first bell at a quarter to eight, loud, triumphant, eager. It was a boy come to pay a bill for which my father had to go downstairs for just a minute to the office. And then I knew all of a sudden that no one would come, no one! It was no compelling and unreasoned premonition, no mysterious prophetic voice, no, it was a perfectly logical deduction from our greasy oil lamp, from my father's shirt-sleeves, from the tip that the boy would get, from the sand strewn over the signature on the receipt stamp. I did not dare look at anyone. I had sympathized so intensely with them that the strings had suddenly snapped; the uncertainty and the feeling of inferiority that had tormented them stabbed me now. I was overwhelmed by the fathomless fear of the dependent child that cannot interfere when his parents are threatened. I also felt a sharp pity for my sister, something I had never known before. Perhaps this is the moment, if there are such moments, when I took leave of childhood, put away childish things and became an adult. And then it was all over as suddenly as it had begun, and I imagined so stubbornly how: "He that is our God is the God of salvation," and the rest of

Psalm 68, verse 20, to an air sprung from Mr. Balkom's brain would yet resound through our rooms that, when the second bell rang, I already prepared myself to make a bow to Lady Sticks whom I saw sweeping in in a sort of trailing garment. This time it was a peasant woman who came to buy a yard and a half of tape at the last minute.

The half hour that followed is something I would rather not remember, it is charged with ominous tragedy far surpassing my own sombre anticipations. Little things particularly, magnified in my memory into blows of fate, struck me deeply. It was something almost repulsive to see my father in his best coat, by means of which he wanted to force the situation, creeping through the rooms, not farther away than two steps into the inviolate front room and hear him mumbling: "They'll be coming, dear." Although I had done it all beforehand, I got busy on my home-work, already without pulling up my trousers when I sat down, and my mother stood idly by the sausages. My sister had been running around the whole house like a hunted animal as if they were all hidden somewhere and it was not until she had hastily thrown on a coat and gone to a friend who lived a few doors from us and was one of the mezzo sopranos, that we really knew where we stood.

"Oh! then it has been put off a week," said my father soberly when my sister had gone upstairs. 'If she didn't know about it, well then . . . . It has been put off a week,' he repeated to my mother who had come out with the sausages and handed me a cake that tasted like sand, 'Nel, Gerrit Barendse's daughter had a notice.'

"And not Fietje?"

"A misunderstanding . . . ."

The next morning in the midst of a vivid dream of my sister and Andersen's little mermaid swimming underwater to lay flowers on a row of church pews, I was awakened by my mother who stuck her head in the door:

"Be a little quiet, Henk, Sophie isn't well." I jumped out of bed and followed her up the hall to ask for details. Putting her finger on her lips she disappeared into my sister's bedroom. I noticed I had a splitting headache. Before I went to school my mother told me that at breakfast Sophie had read an explanatory letter from Lady Sticks but had then felt sick and could not stay up. She gave me a mournful description of the vomiting and all the rest in keeping with her melancholy nature. My father was not at home. Most likely his carefree, cheerful character had made him flee the house, the new chilly neatness of the rooms that made them all look like waiting-rooms. But that I was to continue to be forbidden the sick-room seems to have been a miscalculation. After dinner my mother brought me a request from Sophie to come and "keep her company." With a strange feeling of embarrassment I went upstairs on tiptoe and hesitated even after I had turned the doorknob. The odour of that girl's room was like the smell around a death bed; the doctor and the pharmacist's boy had been there and my mother sprinkled lavender water on such occasions. I had to walk all the way around the bed and bump myself twice before I got to see the patient's face that was not pale as I had expected, but deeply flushed, and above the embroidered high-necked nightgown, perhaps even more beautiful than the evening before.

What she often did, stretch out her right hand palm up with the thumb out to the side, had something commanding, but also a theatrical touch in it that I was conscious of when I sat down beside her bed. "Henk," she said in a loud voice that made me involuntarily look around toward the open door, "You are the only one who must know. I'm not sick. I lied to them. You are the only one who can help me. But you must first read this letter, Henk."

Hereupon she handed me a large sheet of paper that I fingered. A faint, sneaky water-mark interrupted here and there in a most elegant manner made more impression on me than the much more distinct coat of arms. I spelled out in a personal scrawl that hurt my eyes and made me see not the muscular lady with her candle-grease cheeks but all at once the Irish setter belonging to her brother who did not bow. "Miss, It has come to our ears through a trustworthy source that you have more than once been seen in the evening on the edge of our city in the company of a scholar. Without wishing to pronounce judgment on your behaviour in this present case, we nevertheless consider ourselves, after long reflection, not justified in assigning you a solo part in our Christmas cantata. In the name of the committee. A.M.M. Strick van Landsweer."

I remained speechless, sitting with the paper in my hand. This piece was far beyond my slight experience of life. Perhaps I hardly knew what a scholar was and was inclined to think of one of our teachers instead of a schoolboy. Meanwhile the silence became oppressive. Sophie took the letter from me and hid it away. At last I said stupidly:

"Is that Lady Sticks?"

"Who else?" she burst out, pounding on the covers and violently rocking her whole upper body. "Such an insult! It will kill me. If you don't help I shall drown myself!"

"No, don't do that," I stammered awkwardly very much disturbed; but she suddenly grabbed my hand and pulled me towards her bursting into tears. I smelled hair, lavender; I felt a wet warm cheek. I was confused. I still know very well that I was chiefly touched by the evidence of her trust and her not speculating on my sympathy by letting me think she was sick. Luckily just then my mother's voice was heard from below. I jumped up and went to the door; behind me I heard Sophie whisper: "Say it's doing me good!"

After passing this message on to my mother, who called up that I must not tire Sophie, I walked back to my chair, wishing for more light on the mystery. This light was as dismaying as it was unexpected. With wide eyes, turning herself to face me my sister asked:

"Do you know Hugo Verwey?"

She continued to look at me, but instinctively careful to keep a secret that under other circumstances and better prepared I might have been glad to confide to her I did not say a word. This precaution was entirely unconscious. My feeling of utter emptiness and unreality was enough to make me not show anything. The Hugo Verwey stripped something in me bare and crippled something in me. Without a thought I remained staring into space, not even making a connection between that name and the scholar with whom my sister had shown herself on the outskirts of our town and who was to blame for Lady Sticks's letter. Sophie seemed to take for granted that I knew him, that at least I gradually understood. She was talking now very fast and it was only afterwards I was able to piece together the scraps I caught. About two weeks before Hugo Verwey had addressed her on the street; as she felt sorry for his physical defect, and as she could tell from his behaviour that he was not just anybody, she had let herself be persuaded and had walked along with him; his being at the classical school and saying he knew me was also a point of contact. After that she had met him twice more, always in the evening. He had not hidden his age from her nor yet his status of scholar though neither of these could be much of a recommendation to a girl of nearly twenty. As far as I could judge she was very much under the spell of his charm, but it goes without saying that the acquaintance was far too short for what might be called a more intimate contact. I am now positive of this; at the time I did not even think of such a possibility. What interested me much more was who had seen and betrayed them, a question Sophie was just as unable to answer though I recalled Boudewijn Evertsen's remark about what Veenstra or Desmet had shouted about my sister. Only much later, having learned the relationships in our little town and chiefly taking account of the animosity in the cloth guild did I reach a conclusion. Just as my parents felt themselves kicked by the burgomaster, the jonkheer or the judge, the cotton yardage Jews in the shopping street had it in for my father because he cut them on the street; besides — and this seems to me conclusive in this case — there had once been a Sarah Polak black-balled out of the choir who must have been a sister or a cousin of Rusman's! So the line from Rusman to Hugo Verwey, whose attention he may have drawn to my pretty sister, ran back, after those three walks, from Hugo Verwey to Rusman, to Sarah to Rebecca to . . . fill in yourself, Lady Acheron; this seems to me to be the diagram of that slander; but who in the world was the trustworthy source? Oh! let us suppose that the pair had been reported by others; let us suppose that it was the jonkheer's Irish setter.

When my sister thought I had understood everything she kept on looking at me with those same wide open eyes as if she expected something from me, an explosion of wrath or another long speech to console her or to justify the "conduct" of my "fellow scholar." I felt vaguely that our whole school was involved, the classical school that until recently Sophie had so proudly ignored; but actually I did not do much more than repeat to myself: Hugo Verwey, Hugo Verwey, half stunned by the inner surprise of someone else having pronounced his name . . . ..

"You must go to him," said Sophie at last with determination.

I was startled; now at last I took it all in, although I still did not grasp the meaning of the commission with which she seemed to want to charge me. Was it fear, or joy or embarrassment that brought the blood to my cheeks? No, it was not the desire to come to my sister's rescue, but the offer of a chance to come in contact with him that made me tingle all over. And yet I knew I would never dare; I knew I must not take this burden on myself however much I longed to do so with one half of my being.

"What must I do then?" I stammered confusedly to win time. Her eyes flashed angrily at me; then, after a hopelessly resigned lifting of her eye-brows, she set her mouth and jaw and with stubborn patience began to explain to me that the only possible way she could be reinstated was for Hugo Verwey to go to Lady Sticks, or another member of the committee, with an explanation that would remove all suspicion about those evening walks. To my question as to why she did not write to him or go to him herself she answered that she did not know where he lived, that they had not arranged to meet again after the last walk; that she did not wish to expose herself again. In a trembling voice, afraid she might guess my real fear, I told her Hugo's address that I had heard by chance. Just like a student he lived in lodgings in a side street not so very far from us, and I continued to insist that she should write to him at that address, and explain everything and that then everything would be all right and she would be able to sing with the choir again. She nodded agreement with those eager words; but then, whether because I did not say anything about Hugo himself and acted just as if I had never seen him or because of the feeble way I got out of fulfilling her request, she seemed greatly disappointed in me. I was still far from having taken sides when I at last left the room, glad to escape from the conflict. Nor had my sympathy for Sophie easily let itself be neutralized in that solution of rivalry, familiarity, egotism and teasing, the usual dividing and binding medium between brothers and sisters. And still less did it occur to me that I must wipe out the stain on her good name, because the offenders were so unassailably far and grown up, so revered, and congenial like the Reverend Kalmans (whom I counted one with the committee of the choir), so aristocratic like Lady Sticks, while that other vaguer offender in the background was the most unassailable of all.

When after a week, during which before and after school I saw Hugo Verwey like a dangerous young god limping past without taking any notice of me, nothing had changed in Sophie's condition I understood that I was not yet through with her. As our parents had to be kept in ignorance, she had decided to remain sick until her reputation was cleared. This was really the best line of conduct for her, our old kindhearted house doctor, who had brought us all into the world, was in the plot. I did not go much to the sickroom, but the fifth day after the tragic failure of the evening gathering the bomb burst. Sophie's face was very pale now and tense, her hands plucked at the covers like a typhus patient's, she swallowed a couple of times and then handed me another letter, a thin carelessly folded small sheet this time, that smelled of cigarettes. The writing was careless too but pointed and precise in which I read the following:

"Dear Madam. To my regret it is impossible for me to comply with your request. Aside from the fact that I do not know or wish to know the lady you mentioned, I refuse to defend my conduct before such imaginary or self-constituted judges. That would be the way to recognize the rights of the lower middle class. Moreover, my reputation is such that the noble lady would probably not believe a word of my statement. I can only hope that you will look upon this incident with the same contempt as I do. Sunt pueri pueri peurilia trachant. In conclusion I assure you that I have the pleasantest recollections of our evening walks. Respectfully, Your obedient servant, Hugo Verwey."

It was a perfidious document from the young god; but of course I did not see through him; for me he remained where he was: on his pedestal. The unexpressed accusation of being lower middle class including my sister, the cowardly withdrawal, the affable reference to the walks as if to a salesgirl, which now make up one of the bitterest memories, were all lost on me. I was merely impressed by the cool clear language, the unfamiliar turns of phrase, the arrogant Latin, and above all anxious about what would follow. Still pale and tense Sophie in a weak voice whispered that I must tear up the letter. I put it in my pocket with the intention of reading it over five times. I still did not think of taking sides.

"You must go to him, Henk," I heard her muttering.

With head bent I remained staring at my feet and slowly detached my thoughts from the letter. I knew how stubborn she was; I knew too that she had every right to appeal to me; moreover, I had felt all this coming on for days. Before I was fully aware of it I had consented, but not out of any joyful self-sacrificing chivalry. It was a sentence being carried out through me. I was the power of an avenging goddess, willless, like King Gunther when he was ordered to kill Siegfried. It surprised me that Sophie did not read my consent in my face. Why, I wondered, is she bending over so desperately, wringing her hands so theatrically, when she really has got the mastery over me? Why is she talking about the water again? I was inexpressibly relieved when she stopped her convulsive movements that I hardly dared to watch.

"So you'll do it Henk?"

"Yes," I answered dully.

"Do you promise?" "Yes." "You mustn't ask him if he will go to Lady Sticks, but to the parson. I hate her to much." "And if he won't?" "Then . . . " She stopped, pulled me towards her with a broad gesture, so that I stood against her, leaning over the edge of the bed like a horse at a trough, and blushing she finished her sentence: "Then you must avenge me. Do you promise me that? Will you swear it?"

Her words tickled my ear as if I had a lot of little hairs in it. The word avenge which I only knew from tales of Indians meant absolutely nothing to me. But to swear was better, and I would probably have obliged her even if she had talked Greek to me, just to get it over with, to rid of the feeling of the hard board against my knees and no doubt for a lot of other reasons. Because, however stifled and uncomfortable I was in that embrace in which I finally swore, now that I look back on it I realize that the whole situation had the character of a sensual event that must have moved me deeply. Unawakened as I was, my soul has carried that near awakening, that ought to have been an awakening, to this very day and imagination provides what the reality was still too young to know. I still see my long since dead sister before me, as a girl with her black shining eyes, her flushed cheeks and firm chin pressing me against her and trapping me in the odours of her bed just as unconscious of all this as myself. But, however it was, I had sworn.

"Big Henk?" asked Mr. Kalmans turning his cheerful, blond face with its van Dyk beard towards Henk Evertsen, bobbing a little up and down on his toes which always made him so young and athletic, so free from all solemnity even if it was a little like a marionette. Henk Evertsen did not hesitate a second:

"Love of course, Sir!"

"Good," said Mr. Kalmans, and then slowly, by way of a few boys from the trade school and Gerard Steierman, he came to me. It was a long, bare room in which these questions were posed. Only a pale map of Palestine illuminated by the yellow gaslight stood out on one of the walls. On chair seats that had doubtless held many heavy vestry men before they were found to be only good enough for the catechism local, we sat with the usual comfortable informality in this place not known officially as disorder; but I really was not sitting with them although I knew for certain that I would not say "love". I saw everything

60

through a mist. I had not slept for two nights. What awaited me after this hour of catechism I did not want to think of; but that I should not say "love" that was in any case the least requirement, the first step. If I once practised being grown-up then the boy would vanish automatically. That was the only reason I had wanted to wait until after the weekly catechism lesson with Mr. Kalmans, who was connected with the church choir and so bore a part of the blame, and to whom Hugo Verwey must go according to my sister's will, law for me, since I had sworn. Although I was normally fond of Mr. Kalmans all my hate was concentrated on him. I scarcely knew Lady Sticks by sight, besides she was titled. But my sister lay in bed, and my father slept restlessly and kept asking what was to be done about the choir and twice a day I was being called to the sick-room to be reminded of something. No, "love"—I'd be darned if I would.

"Jard?" asked Mr. Kalmans in a genial tone. He had been somewhat delayed by the trade school boys with black smears on their faces who got mixed up in their definitions.

"Love, Sir."

What was being asked was a definition of God. These definitions were the nicest things about the catechism lessons because they made us think for ourselves and sometimes argue with Mr. Kalmans and therefore I was disappointed in the midst of all my misery that Gerard Steierman could not think of any more original answer than "love", which all the others down to the dullest fisherman's son had already proclaimed, the result moreover of last week's instruction. I remember one evening when Gerard, almost against his own better judgement had out of theism, deism, pantheism chosen the last, his chief argument being that "if God was everywhere he really did not exist at all," and besides that Mr. Kalmans made the confusion still worse by asking if pantheism had anything to do with the heathen god Pan, all in good faith of course. Unfortunately, Mr. Kalmans, even when he contradicted you most emphatically, always ended by agreeing with you in some complicated way without putting himself in the wrong, which in the long run had a disarming effect and after all, I could not blame Gerald Steierman if love were less inspiring than pantheism.

"Little Henk?" asked Mr. Kalmans.

That was me. I waited a second then I said slowly and bluntly.

"In any case not love."

61

I learned later that Mr. Kalmans had not known anything about the affair Sophie, let alone taken part in it; as he was known as a liberal he had been kept out of the obscurantist action of the choir committee. But, although there was nothing in his manner to indicate that he realized he was facing an enemy, for me the victory was complete. In my overwrought condition he looked to me stupid, superficial, smirking, ready for conciliatory words; but he would not catch me. A murmur of surprise had spread along the rows of chairs; Gerald Steierman's steady round eyes fixed themselves on me as if something had dawned on him and he wished he could withdraw his answer. I was so dazed from lack of sleep I was not even thinking of Hugo Verwey.

"Hmmm . . . " Mr. Kalmans see-sawed on his toes and pulled at his little fair beard—"have you perhaps another answer, Henk?"

He had spoken calmy, cheerfully, confidingly as if we two were along in that room. Instead of sticking to my negative answer until he has asked for an explanation I began to search for something new that would confound him still more. And so I was trapped and the attack on the God of salvation was no longer difficult to repulse.

"Well?" he asked, see-sawing rather impatiently.

"Justice," I said gruffly, giving the first abstract idea that occured to me. Only abstract ideas counted, that was the conclusion we had agreed on: that God was a quality, a being, not a "person", in spite of the former majority for theism.

"And how do you imagine this God of justice, Henk?" Long silence. Urgently the slender black-clad figure see-sawed up and down, and the gold watch was brought to light, for it was almost eight o'clock and more had to be said about love; otherwise, perhaps Mr. Kalmans would have liked to indulge in a comparison of the God of the New and of the Old Testament. With a friendly, reproachful frown he glanced towards the other end of the table where the murmurs persisted. But I saw nothing of all this and no words formed in my feverish brain; I only felt the draught coldly creeping under doors and gripping my heart. I was feeling the silent chill October evening around me in that long narrow classroom in that small-minded town where the grown-ups were already showing their lack of understanding and their hostile intentions, and in it that one street where I had to go after this sham victory.

"Well boys, I think big Henk really has a better idea! God is, of course, something so mighty and indescribable and can be explained in various ways; but still love . . . A personal, earnest relationship towards God . . . our God . . . "

Outdoors I waved the clamorous questioners away and made haste in the direction of the street where he lived. The moon, almost full, stood above the houses on my right hand. The thin mist that had been blowing about at seven o'clock had cleared. I did not know what was more ominous: the shops that were still open or those already closed. From an untraceable direction a fog horn sounded. Above our dark shop darkness again and above that at the top of the house, the yellow light of Sophie's little bedroom where an oil lamp had been placed. I thought of the sailboat still standing on the floor in the living-room; perhaps it would stand there a while and only rattle again when I had accomplished my task and Sophie was cured. With my teeth chattering from the damp night air, I turned into the first side street I came to; the street I was bound for and that ran parallel to it I reached through a cross alley a few minutes farther on. This second street where I was soon walking without realizing that my goal was now close at hand was narrower than I had thought, rather dark and full of push-carts, and rolls of rope in front of shops. After about twenty steps I noticed in the distance in front of one of the houses a group of two or three people in a dim yellow light; I also thought I caught the sound of voices now and then. Not from fear but because I wanted to be sure of the numbers, I turned back and started again way at the other end of the street where the numbers began. Praying and imploring that the little troupe would not be standing at his door I drew nearer; I never thought for a moment of waiting until they went away. Mechanically, torpidly I counted each house, each workshop I passed, and yet I had made a mistake for there I was where I had to be with Jelte Veenstra's face right in front of me, his drowsy cow-like eyes wide open in the darkness; I did not dare to pay attention to the others. I immediately walked past them in a curve so I could look up unnoticed to where the light came from and where his room must be. There was gas light there and a few gilt picture frames against dark wallpaper. Behind me their voices resumed the conversation, remote, businesslike, unmindful of me. When I turned around the voices stopped. A hostile silence reigned, six or seven steps away from me. Next to Jelte Veenstra is was not Charles Desmet or Rusman I perceived, but a boy in the sixth

63

class called Lodyzer, also one of our imports and of the foulest kind, a bloated, short, fat fellow with bad teeth. The third was Hugo Verwey without hat or cap; the light fell directly on his dark brown, curly hair that had a tinge of red in it. I saw he was standing with his legs crossed, but they did not show any defect, any malformation, and the way he held his right hand with his wrist bent behind the lapel of his brown jacket looked lordly and graceful. As I knew Jelte Veenstra the best of the two others I addressed him.

"Does Hugo Verwey live here?"

Coming closer I smelled liquor on his breath; he mumbled something: the others said nothing. With a loathing I asked the vulgar Lodyzer.

"Does Hugo Verwey live here?"

Lodyzer looked over my shoulder towards the end of the street and slowly, very slowly drew a wooden pipe out of one of his trouser pockets and pointed with its stem at the third man whom I still had not dared to look in the face. Then he stuck the pipe in his mouth and sucked air through it smacking his lips.

At this moment something happened that completely distracted my attention. The humming of Jelte Veenstra who seemed to be half drunk had gradually turned into a gutteral singing: one line from an unknown text stupidly repeated over and over.

"What a tasty lady's body!"

He sang it seriously and with a certain candour. But the words with that grotesque emphasis on y's were the tune, which was that of a popular street song, rose pertly to a high note and then fell again, seemed so abject to me that I felt the earth sinking beneath me. While Lodyzer with his pipe between his teeth began to laugh, Hugo Verwey took a step forwards.

"What have you come for?"

"I just want to speak to you a minute," I answered timidly with my eyes fixed on the ground; now that I was not looking at him he seemed to be made of granite, broadshouldered, and ever so much larger than myself, although in reality he only came a little above the shoulder of tall Jelte Veenstra.

"But I don't even know you."

Of course he knew I was Sophie's brother. Besides, had he not told her once himself that he knew me? It would have made everything much easier for me if I had called his attention to the contradiction, in a casual way bringing in Sophie's name which from that beginning had seemed the most difficult thing to do, and then like this in the presence of that company? But to have been able to think out such a thing I would have had to be less surprised at his voice which I had never before heard distinctly and which, however musical and softly lilting, was easily heard above the continued braying of Jelte Veenstra. Hanging on to that unexpected voice, I looked beseechingly at him and was still more encouraged by the absence of the usual provoking line around the corners of his mouth. No disdain was apparent on that narrow, motionless face whose features seemed carved in some delicately spotted luminous metal-like material. It was a face composed of rosy, ribbed shells overlapping each other, eyelids, the pouches under the eyes, the blunt nose, a seaworthy face, delicate and yet weathered, repellent and at the same time indescribably alluring there in the dark under that yellow light from his room.

"I don't know you," he repeated quietly.

"May I speak to you alone?" I asked in a shaky voice, doing my very best not to listen to that disgusting song or to Lodyzer's chuckling, but concentrating entirely on him. He threw his head back a little and crossed his arms over his chest.

"If it is about that letter then not."

Here Lodyzer broke in.

"Well you had better believe it, Hugh, she is sending you . . . . . "

"You must realize I won't take orders, Mannoury," said Hugo Verwey, without paying attention to the others in a much louder voice than at first. "If I make the acquaintance of someone I don't wish to be punished by being sent to a lady."

"But there's no need of that," I stammered eagerly, stretching my hand out towards him. "Better not actually—If you will just go to the Reverened Kalmans to tell him . . . . ."

The others seemed to have waited for this. Jelte Veenstra broke off his song about the lady's body and let out a low rumbling laugh, gently swaying his colossal rump while Lodyzer jabbed the air with his pipe and shouted: 'That's good. Reverend Kalmans! That's darned good! Reverend Kalmans did he say! Ho, ho, ho, ho!'

They danced and swayed; back of me on the right I saw their big, cowardly shadows moving back and forth. But nevertheless I held on to the idea of an audience with Hugo Verwey. Just one surge of anger and then I was once more suspended on his lips. He had not laughed, he did not even have a mocking look, rather there was something like pity in his ruddy brown face.

"That does not make any difference to me," he said. "So you won't do it?" I asked submissively, on the point of turning around, away at least from that dreadful noise behind me.

Suddenly it stopped (it seemed to have been produced only by Lodyzer; Jelte Veenstra had swallowed the wrong way and was hiccupping at intervals) and Lodyzer advanced, gesticulating with his pipe he explained:

"If she wants to marry you, Hugh, then I'll bear witness that she . . . " and he ended with an obscenity that I have by no means forgotten but that will not appear here. I turned around and kicked him with all my might in the groin, so that he staggered back howling and remained standing doubled over with his hands on his belly. I had not spoken or shouted. But all this had happened in such a flash that the feeling of humility towards Hugo Verwey had not had time to disappear; no transition was taking place in me; I was falling apart into two halves; but even in that brief instant a logical connection must have arisen between these two domains; my fury and my slavish servitude, because I can still remember very well that I felt I was fighting not for my insulted sister, but for him; and not to show him my courage or my highly developed sense of honour, but to defend him, heaven knows from what . . .

Just as Jelte Veenstra, who was leaning against a pillar of the porch, started his song again between two hiccups and I began to feel in my own belly the sickening, deathly sensation felt by the writhing figure (I knew it from experience), a hand was laid on my shoulder. I looked into a distorted face and heard the almost sobbing words: "I'll teach you, little fool." I received two or three slaps on my cheeks with the flat of the hand, not very hard; two hands bent me over forwards and a sharp but impelling kick on my seat sent me to my knees in front of the porch of the next house. He must have done it with his left leg, the one that was not lame. I remained in that position for nearly half a minute expecting more. When I stood up tears were running down my face, but the door was already closed, the street empty. High above me, out of his room where the curtains had been drawn, their hushed voices sounded. Whenever those voices got a little louder I shivered, but I stayed there not knowing where to go. To sleep on the same floor with Sophie was impossible. The interview with him still had to take place; there was no help for it; I had come here for that; for that I was staying because now I only remembered the disturbance caused by Jelte Veenstra and Lodyzer and scarcely at all his refusal. I crossed the street and concealed myself in the entrance to an alley from where I could keep my eye on the house. As soon as the two others had gone I would ring the door bell and ask again to speak to him.

When the moon had already climbed so high that its light on one side of the walls of the narrow alley was within arms reach, I heard a trampling on the stairs and the door was flung open. Two figures stepped out into the darkness of the street, first Jelte Veenstra, quite sober judging by his gait, then Lodyzer who seemed to be limping and then after a little longer interval, a third. I realized then that the limping one must be Hugo Verwey accompanying the others. Lodyzer, who had closed the door behind him was walking normally, not even being supported. When they were ten houses farther on I crept out of my hiding place intending to follow them at a distance. A tower clock close by struck nine. At first I was sleepy and chilled from my long vigil against the wall, but the motion and the passing scenery cleared my head. To make sure they were still walking ahead of me, I occasionally bent far forward and saw their heads in relief against the clear moonlight on the houses across the street, where not far from our corner there was a curve with staring white-painted facades. But this background also slid past and they were about to turn into our street. Hugo limped along in the middle as if between two seconds. He wore neither a cap nor an overcoat; it had become remarkably balmy since the fog had cleared. Posted behind a push-cart I saw them linger at the corner; hands were shaken; I caught the sounds of leave-taking; then Jelte Veenstra, recognizable by his height, disappeared to the right while the other two took the left. I ran on my toes to the left corner to make sure they would not escape me up another side street; but that impulse can be ascribed even more to the joy of soon meeting Hugo Verwey alone without a companion. It was plain enough: he was going to see Lodyzer home because he was still in pain, or was no longer in pain — in any case it was natural to see somebody home after such a thing. Under the trees of our street I saw them walking leisurely along, illuminated now and then by street lamps. Again I passed my house with the yellow lamplight in the upper window, the house that banished me until my promise had been kept. But now I was hopeful again; it was only a matter of minutes; I knew where Lodyzer lived, and yes, that was the direction their steps were taking; now they had turned into the street that was the shortest way to the shopping street. Lodyzer lived not far from Rusman.

Hidden in a shallow portico I was entirely dependent on the sounds just around the corner where Lodyzer boarded with a grocer. I could not understand a word; luckily it did not last long. After the door banged I expected to see Hugo walk past me or in any case past the entrance to the side street, but his footsteps receded, mingled with the footsteps of other passers-by and then were gone at the very moment I hesitatingly crept around the corner. One look in the main street told me he must have disappeared. Controlling my despair I first looked for Rusman's home above one of the cloth shops. All was dark. Past the flannel and the unbleached cotton that could not smell now, I ran to the next side street, looking back again and again. Just as I had made sure there was no one walking in that street I heard a door behind me, voices, more farewells; I dodged aside flattening myself against a low somewhat recessed garden gate and listened if the footsteps were approaching or receding. They approached. In a few moments Hugo Verwey limped past my side street and on up the shopping street in the direction of its square-like prolongation which looked dark in the distance and became darker beyond the last street lamp. Behind me on the left the moon was brighter and seemed to drive me out of my course, up against the houses where our shadows fitted along, his bowing and shrinking as if thoughtfully bent over with each halting motion. Even though there were much fewer pedestrians, I felt as though I were still in the centre of the town. Moon and bricks — I did not think of the sea. Little by little and according to a sort of calculation I increased my pace: with every three steps one step nearer. I was about fifty steps behind him; in one hundred and fifty steps I would have caught up; that would take about two minutes. Suddenly, threatening and sullen, there arose in a back-stage light from a dull lemon yellow bracket lamp, the old city gate where the sailors always stood spitting and the yellow butcher's dogs lay on the cobblestones. Not one was standing or lying there. The distance between us was no more than fifteen steps when without a backward glance, his shoulder momentarily shining brown in the lamp-light, he disappeared into the dark opening of the gate. The coat-of-arms above the gate shrank, two crossed hands became flabby empty gloves; I too had hurried into the gate fully prepared to run into him at the other side. I forgot all precaution; my fear, my despair were left behind; I did not know what I would say to him, but because it was dark there I should not mind being slapped or kicked again. A cool west wind, a damper air, the tail end of the wink of the elegant lighthouse announced the sea. Unexpectedly I saw him now at the left on the way to the little harbor flanked by two short piers which hardly deserved the name silted up as it was. Fishing boats never came in more than half way, the other half was only navigable for row boats which were usually moored there, owned in common by the population, particularly the young. A half-grown boy had only to make friends with any loitering fisherman, and he had the use of one of these boats. At least all the boys of the classical school were exempted from paying, even damages were not charged to them. While I followed Hugo across the sandy stretch that led to the northern pier stumbling over pieces of wood and loose barbed wire, I still had not the vaguest suspicion of what he intended to do. The moon shone so bright that beyond the mouth of the harbour a bluish silver lane could be followed almost to the horizon, but out there a far thin mist prevailed, drawn up by the moon, blown back by the wind or perhaps arising spontaneously from the ambiguous rising and falling water round about the Gravel Bar lying half an hour's rowing out at sea and flooding over at high tide. Although I had been there often enough, the sand bar took on a more mysterious significance than before, only because the sea lay open so unexpectedly far in that direction, even though not directly illuminated like the sparkling water of the harbour where the limping figure of Hugo Verwey moved along. But not until he began to descend one of the roughly cut stairs in the stone at the beginning of the harbour did I understand that he too must feel drawn to the mysterious changeable island in the midst of the sea. Perhaps he longed for cool space, for spray on his cheeks, after the company he had just left.

Behind a bulging black and white painted mooring post smelling of tar I made myself small to wait for what he was going to do. It was a strange sight to see that crippled figure step into one of the boats, fasten one of the oars and push off with the other. The water rippled out to both piers and in the deserted harbour the splash of the oars was the only sound. He was rowing now rather quickly. He might be away an hour, or less, but also half the night until the moon went down. I could not wait here. And before I had asked him my question the second time I could not go home either. That is why I decided to follow him in one of the other boats, to watch him, to speak to him on the Gravel Bar out at sea; (it was not because I would be safe from another dressing-down that this plan appealed to me, but because I was becoming gradually conscious of the romance of it); or at the worst I would return in his wake and after that I could accost him on the shore. When the rhythmical splashing at the mouth of the harbour had died away, I hurried along the same road he had taken towards the boat lying most in shadow and began to be filled with reckless self-confidence. The firmer my decision became the more I felt delivered from the despair that had gripped me during my march through the town. Far out at sea he could no longer despise me; that was impossible. He would understand how in earnest I was and that I could not do otherwise for Sophie's sake. He would esteem me for my daring; he would not be able to refuse me anything. Finally, I might bring him back to Sophie's feet . . . . In a fever I untied the rope and stepped into the boat. The water was falling, in an hour it would be ebb tide; the distance between the high water mark on the stone steps to the surface of the sea below was more than a metre. I tried to row faster than he had done. Under my bent knees an oblong of bilge water swung back and forth later to be illuminated by the moon like a knight's shield carried with me. Pulling hard on the oars I could almost have shouted for joy; but once out of the harbor with the first full flashes of the lighthouse on my left, I kept looking over my shoulder so as not to catch up with him too quickly.

My jubilant mood lasted the first ten minutes of my trip to the Gravel Bar; after that things got more and more confused and my memory can no longer quite recapture them. Water spattering around me, the singing wind, the creaking of the oars together formed the accompaniment of my joy. From one end of the horizon to the other the lighthouse rolled its eye. I had to keep a somewhat southerly course, because of the current. I very nearly loved the sea because it was no sea, but moonlight on the sea and in it two who were going to find each other. But there my sleepless nights, how many indeed, went to my head like wine, suddenly, uncontrollably; I thought I would topple over, but I rowed on and when I turned around I felt the wind full in my face and scanned the horizon mechanically where the yellowish grey line gently lapped by the water must soon appear. I didn't see his boat, but where else could he have gone than to the Gravel Bar? And if he was not there then I would pretend he was: limping, hopping like a light brown insect on that curved bank with its shining shells that got smaller and disappeared when the tide came in to emerge again when it ebbed six hours later; and then he would still be there waiting for me so we could at last tell each other everything that united our hearts. Weren't we both good oarsmen? Weren't we both at the Classical School? No, not that distorted face, Hugo Verwey, not those scornful words! Away with that coppery face that waylaid me here to hold me back, threatening, searching, accusing, and then it was gone; faded into the outline of the sand bar that I mounted with the murmuring waves. Perhaps we would all three yet sing in Mr. Kalmans' church choir in the hard stalls and I would retract all my objections to the God of Love. If his boat was not there — but his boat was indeed there, although there was no sign of himself on that low island, now probably at its largest, fifteen minutes' walk in circumference. Just as I felt my boat grounding I noticed the long black shape on my right not very far away. The boat lay there without being fastened with a rope to an iron pile: he must know too that the tide was now out and would only be high in six hours. The moon shone from high in the sky on the gentle slope sprinkled with constellations of shells; I let my own boat go ashore between two of them and there lay the two boats on the sand as if they would never more be parted. If he was not on the island then I would of course have to take his boat back with me to let him see what I could do . . . Yes, I had to do that, it had to be done and what need had he of a boat? It seemed to me harder than anything in the world, but perhaps I did it automatically. My hands were all set to do it; it was the last task I had to accomplish to find peace, to be able to sleep. Where was the painter? Was it long enough? How queer, those oars I did not need and could lay down carefully on one side. To shove his boat back into the water, fasten the rope at the right place on my boat and then get both boats afloat was splendid exercise, and only now did I notice the lighthouse waving back to me from far off. Yes, I was coming. The wind was with me. The wind blew across the island and dried it, it blew again and brought the waves with it. I was coming. He could not stay there forever limping in the moonlight. If he wanted to come back I would go and get him by the same road; but first his boat must be brought to safety. Or perhaps he would not even want to go along for what friends did he have on land? In any case, I had defended him against his enemies. At school he would now have a quiet life with me, and he would know all, understand all . . . . How the wind followed me now, playing with his boat that dragged on mine, and scarcely cooling my forehead. Everything seemed so peaceful, a good end. And yes, there was the lighthouse still, half it size and here right before my eyes the second boat, pointing to the left or right, left or right of the position where the ever shrinking sand bar lay or maybe once straight at it and then, whenever I looked around, the lighthouse again at whose base I could at last go to sleep, when the lights went out in the early morning, in the town, six hours later.

No, he did not drown though no one could have hoped he would be saved any more than I did during those days when our old doctor spoke of brain fever and a consultation and observation. Day and night my sister sat beside me until she too had to go to bed really sick this time. And the Christmas cantata was so completely driven out of our minds by all this that it was not even mentioned when I went back to school and heard how it all ended. No one ever knew how it really happened, no one ever suspected that it was I who had taken the boat away from the Gravel Bar, not even my sister, in spite of my wild utterances during my delirium. In my semisomnambulistic state I had brought the two boats back to the harbor where they were found still fastened together; but as far as I know no investigation was ever made. All that was talked about was the miraculous rescue. Hugo Verwey was said to have fought like a hero against the rising tide, for hours and hours, first with his clothes on, then naked, swimming or standing on tip-toe where shells gave solid footing. At five in the morning he was seen by fishermen, and exhausted and benumbed he was brought in in a row boat. Pneumonia followed and a cure at Davos; and it may very well be that he is still alive, although he never came back to our town. I am still proud that he acquitted himself so well in that element I hate because after all he was my friend. And it was only because he was my friend that I did what freed me from a passion that left no room for myself. Anyone who thinks I took the boat away in revenge, revenge for my sister or revenge for the castigation he administered to me has not understood my story and perhaps that is the best way to read it, the best way also for myself, who for years afterwards up until I was twenty or twenty-one and my feeling for him had long since disappeared still had to suffer the punishment of dreaming of Hugh Verwey: how I rowed after him, caught up with him, lay beside him on an endless golden beach, where supernatural voices sang far above our heads, where there was no place for parting, no road back to the city whither I alone had fled.

BUSTER

ALAN BURNS

BUSTER

Buster:
A small new loaf or large bun
A thing of superior size or astounding nature
A burglar
A spree
A dashing fellow
A Southerly gale with sand or dust
A piece of bread and butter
A very successful day
Hollow, utterly, low
To fall or be thrown

(Dictionaries).

They stood over him.

Grandma shrieked:

"Let me look at you! What a big boy you've grown! Have a chocolate! Have a pear! Have some more seedcake darling! You're not eating anything! How can you be a big man without eating anything? What is he going to be when he grows up?"

"Lord Chief Justice," said his father.

"Prime Minister" said Grandma. "Danny, who do you like better, your mother or your father?"

"Both the same," he said.

That night he wrapped the sheets round it, then a mountain of blankets, then the eiderdown tucked in. Small pig hot inside. Then wet.

In the bath his mother had told him never play with that. Never. It's dirty. It will make you go mad, like being bitten by a frothy dog. Told him again and again how his cousin had stood up to make himself soapy, but his heel felt the curve of the bath and his spine cracked the edge of the bath and the nerve was crushed and the bone splintered and the track for the nerve from the brain to the legs was ruined and he sits in a chair all day now. Dan had seen those legs in their grey flannel trousers, skinny knees poking through like pins.

But this was so easy and lovely. He watched moonlit clouds slide evenly between him and the moon.

His mother's hand held his hand, pointed at the sheets. His face pushed into the smelly sheets.

"You wait till your father comes home. You just wait."

She had locked the dining-room door. He walked slowly round the table squeaking his fingers on the polished wood; he slid his penknife along the grooves, collected threads of dirt. He stood on the window-sill, looked out over the hedge into the road. A soldier posted a letter. He jumped on to the couch, his feet sank in as he pranced about on it. He waited. He reached up for the sweet dish; it fell on the carpet. Liquorice allsorts. He crawled round picking them up: one for the dish, one for his mouth. He poked under the tails of the green monkeys climbing the vase; when the reached the top he'd get a Rolls Royce. He sat on the couch and waited.

He saw the car through the window. Quickly he put his father's slippers in front of the big chair. It was his job. He banged on the door.

"Let me out!"

He wanted to be first, to run down the path, be swung up on to the garden wall, given a piggyback. The door stayed shut. He heard them talking. He kicked the slippers across the room. They lay in the empty fireplace. They were black and red tartan wool.

Upstairs to the spare room, his father treading behind. He pulled his trousers down, they wouldn't come over his shoes.

"That's enough!"

He hobbled to the bed, lay across it. The prickles of the hairbrush touched his bottom.

"Get up and get dressed. You'll go straight to bed without supper."

He heard them arguing. His mother brought him snap crackle pop with milk.

He heard his brother coming up the stairs. He bounced up and down making the bedsprings prink. Bryan came in, sat on the bed, smiled, waited.

"I hate her," Dan said.

"You shouldn't. She's your mother."

"She's got sticking-out eyes and frizzy hair."

"That's only because she's not got enough iodine."

There was an old brown photo of her kissing under an orange tree.

"I'm a cruiser with six-inch guns," Bryan said, "and father's a battleship and mother's the Ark Royal stuffed with tuck instead of planes."

"What about me?"

"Oh you're nothing. You don't want to be in this fleet."

"I do."

"Well you're a brilliant destroyer, the fastest ship in the Navy. And you've got torpedoes which can sink anything."

"Where are we going?"

"We're steaming across the Bay of Biscay to fight for Spain."

"Then what happens?"

"Tell you tomorrow. Go to sleep."

"Now."

"Tomorrow. Good night, sleep well."

"Goodnight. I don't want to be Lord Chief Justice."

"You haven't got to be."

"They all say I will."

"Never mind them. Good night whippersnapper."

"Night."

2

Bryan was home all day because he had finished school and not found a job yet. They played french cricket in the garden and read a story in *The Wizard* about U-boats and Dan made a speech in Parliament:
"Why should the rich have pears and cake and the poor can't even have bread?"

Bryan said: "Hooray!"

Boys came round and they held Dan between them and raced him along the street, flying him into the air.
"Let me down! Let me down!"

But when they stopped, he cried: "Do it again!"
"Come in and listen to the wireless. Sh! It's important."

Mr. Chamberlain. The war had started. The air-raid siren went. Dan got under the dining-room table. His mother was making tea; she bent down and looked in:
"You all right down there?"

He hugged the cross-piece between his legs. He was nine.

They were talking about boarding school.

His father said: "It's too much for you dear. Bryan can look after himself. But the other one."

His father stood at the foot of the bed:
"I'm sorry Dan. It's the war. We didn't know there was going to be a war did we?"
"Here's a pound for spends," his father was shouting as the train moved off.
"What?"
"Not what, pardon. Look after your mother and write every week."

Staring out of the train windows. Boring. Just fields. Reading *Woman* and *Melody Maker* with mother.

Strange roads. Greygravel path. Grey walls. Eyesocket staring windows. Standing while mother mumbled with Headmaster. Unbroken tradition. Evacuated. Discipline. Horseriding and Music extra. Tall boy walked slowly past the open door, twisting his head to stare. Matron. Cash's name tapes. Down a corridor, clicking a radiator. Mother grabbed his arm. Corridors leading off. Hundreds of doors. He would never find his way around.

"He will have to be inspected."

Trousers down round his ankles, getting creased. Hobbling, taking the fawn rug with him over the slidy floor. Mother getting up to help.

Doctor roaring: "He'd better get used to undressing himself!"

The carefully balanced timetable cut up the days. Mr. Hoffman took Geography. Two sweets after lunch followed by compulsory rest period. Miss Lazarus took French. Desks in rows. Mr. Hoffman walked up and down, sometimes he was in front, sometimes behind your back. Miss Lazarus had a special high desk she had bought herself, in France. Diagrams on the walls. A woman cut through the middle, green kidneys, orange heart. A fat minim, black crotchets, quavers, semi-quavers, demisemiquavers. The British Empire rolled down red, and on a dusty table in the corner a relief map of the neighborhood with cardboard roads and bits of green sponge trees.

He stood on the cold bumpy football field, by the white goal-posts. The others charged around. If only he could dribble right through them and smash the ball into the net. But he was so glad he wasn't one of those who just ran near the ball, shouting, pretending.

Mr. Beezley made Dan sweeping perfect, and in front of everybody showed him how to hold the broom so as not to sweep the dust on to his own shoes. Mr. Beezley took Latin. O table. Smack smack smack smack Dan's eyes went flat on four walls.

Anything could happen on Sunday. He walked through the garden at the back, looked into the greenhouse at the black grapes dangling in bubbled bunches from the green vine spreading out. Over the fence, scratched by rusty wire, down the middle of the road past the chestnut tree with the cobbled wall round it, into a wood he'd never been in before. He sensed the deep heat of autumn, saw it gobbling up the green, scraped thick moss on to his hand. Out into a new wide field, hunting for mushrooms. Hand down in wetness, fingers at the base of the stalk, gentle snap, then peel back a strip of skin to make sure it wasn't a toadstool, nibble a bit. Puffball, puff, brown smoke. He pocketed hazelnuts. He wrenched a stick from the hedge and swiped the hedge with it. He struck the neck of a drooping flower, the dark head slipped off and down into damp dark grass. The split stalk shivered, showed sticky white blood. A tremble fixed his hand, held his stomach, legs, head. Stockstill unbelief. A hawk hovered. He pointed his stick straight at the one pin dangerous eye. At school he was bumped awake. He told them about the fox he had seen close up.

Harry Finegold made him go horseriding. Such tough necks. Dan was too skinny. When the horse chewed grass, shoving his neck down, he couldn't pull him up. Harry Finegold gripped with his knees, got the horse between his legs. Dan sat on top. He trotted, bumping. The horse saw home a half mile down the road, his back hooves slipped as he jerked forward in a sudden gallop. Dan sat straight as a Bengal Lancer. He could not believe he was galloping. Then slowly he slipped sideways.

"Up you get!"

Harry's voice. No.

"You're going to be Prime Minister and you can't even ride a pony!"

He dreamt he was searching for someone among shopping crowds. He caught up with her, she changed, he saw her further on. He held her sleeve, it came away, it was a German, blackclad Germans swung from parachutes, columns of Germans with rifles marched over him. He clung to a bomber's wings, diving into trees, rocketing up, looping through the clouds. And at night he found easier suppler ways, unobtrusive sexy ways. That lovely feel of between, squeezed between his slippery thighs, or under him. And in the garden lavatory, wooden bucket seat, stinking pail, he found old soft sweets, covered himself with them.

He worked at the paino. He held his hands and wrists correctly, tapped each note separate and clear. All Sunday he practiced the first page of his piece.

"Quite good. A little wooden. Go on."

"That's all I've done."

"Better play it right through, even badly."

"What's the use of playing badly? I want to play it brilliantly, perfectly, better than anyone else has ever played it."

At half-term he gave up the piano.

The Headmaster took General Knowledge. He explained about clocks, Parliament, motor cars, the Armed Forces, icebergs, telephones, pollination, traffic lights, Mount Everest expeditions, orchestras, railway engines. It was Dan's best subject. For his Task he gave a talk on the Russian Revolution, and made a colored map to show the dispositions of the Interventionist armies. At home, when his Report came, his father was proud of the second in General Knowledge and told Grandma and Uncle George. That his position in form was twelfth out of fifteen was only because he hadn't settled down yet.

At home Dan missed the countryside, and he walked often in the park. He would whistle *The Trumpet Voluntary* or *The Blue Danube* as loudly and perfectly as he could. Perhaps a composer or a violinist would come up and say: "You whistle very beautifully young man. You have an exceptionally sensitive ear. You must take up music — one day you will be great." Or he sang *The Marseillaise* hoping that a Frenchman would recognize it and reward him for Loyalty to the Republic.

Bryan one morning marched off to the park to help dig trenches and fill sandbags. He held a garden spade riflewise and did a "P-r-e-s-e-n-t Arms!". Dan went to watch. At lunchtime they sat together on a park seat. Bryan tried to rub the clay off his flannels.

"You're the first to know, Dan. I'm joining the Army."

"God! Dad won't let you."

"I must—"

"But Dad says you're doing war-work."

"As his Secretary! Any woman could do the job. I'm nothing. I didn't even go to Spain."

"You weren't old enough."

"It's the same war and I'm old enough now."

"I'm going too."

"You stay at school and work like mad. You're the clever one. You've got a big chance."

Dan wandered round the park, and arrived back at the trenches to go home with his brother. They walked along without speaking. Dan was annoyed: "Why don't you say anything?"

"I'm thinking. And I'm tired."

"But I love having proper conversations with you."

"You can't order 'one conversation' like a pound of apples."

"You talk with Philip all the time."

"We exchange ideas."

Dan was silent. Then, near home, he said:

"Plato did all the talking and the others just said 'Oh yes' or 'I don't agree' to set him off again. I could do that with you."

Bryan said: "Okay. You win. But it's a bit late now."

"Yes. But after the war."

"Of course."

Bryan spoke quietly, coolly, explaining. His mother sobbed: "You mustn't go, you'll get killed, don't go, please, for my sake." His father said: "Why didn't you discuss it with me first? But we understand how you feel. You must do what you think is right." Dan listened.

Bryan's Training Camp was "Somewhere in Scotland". Dan watched him go on the nameless Express. The thread linking their eyes pulled and pulled and snapped. Dan sat with his arms folded. An iron shovel shovelled bricks behind a planked wall of advertisements. Above, dirty panes of tough glass backed by steel netting shut off the sky. On the wide platform people walked in various directions, away from each other, unconnected, yet together making a pattern. Clip clink tread pad in time with tinned music from loudspeakers. Fat pigeons walked among them, heads bobbing out of time with their feet. An unprepared roar and shriek of steam frightened the young ones, made them jump and fly a few yards. The people took no notice. A little boy was dragged along by his mother as she hurried off somewhere; his spare hand wiped his runny nose. Three young soldiers, sweating in thick uniform, drifted by grinning. Whippersnappers raced in and out of telephone boxes, pressing button B. Nuns looked funny and young in light blue, their big white hats turned up like paper gliders. They chatted and nodded. An Irish voice: "It was a wedding present. He picked it out with a pin." Two girls in skyblue shorts were glared at. *I Speak Your Weight* spoke a lady's *Fourteen Stone Four Pounds* to everyone as she giggled. Sticks dropped and bounced on the platform. Porters shoved trolleys loaded with cartons of kippers Deposit Four Shillings. A girl from India stood blinding in orange. The fruit stall was a box on the platform, a spare bit in the train set. A pound of apples, paid for, was left on the counter. A face looked out, then a hand took the bag inside. Men wandered into the Gents' Hairdressing & Brush Up, emerged unchanged. A tramp searched for fag ends; his head was twisted so that his cheek was forced permanently against his shoulder. Ticket collector touched the hands of girls and watched them on to the train. Yorkshireman talked extra loud in London. A kid swung on his father's hand: father smiled wide and lovely. People walked in various directions, away from each other, unconnected, yet together making a pattern.

He took the War Map from Bryan's room to his own. He replaced the little flags on pins which marked the positions of the armies: union jacks, tricolours, swastikas. He stretched colored cotton across the pins to mark the Maginot and Siegfried lines. He cut out a big flag, marked it with a red "B" and stuck it in Scotland.

Bryan sent letters to his brother at school, and in the holidays enclosed a separate note for him in the family letter. Once he mentioned that on his first leave he would "sell a lot of old junk including my bicycle." Dan hauled the bicycle out of the garage, mended the punctures, cleaned the chromium. He looked through the "Wanted" colums of the local newspapers, cycled miles around reading cards in newsagents' windows, and in the end sold it for six pounds which he kept in his brother's room. Another letter advised Dan to:

"do some proper reading. Less newspapers and politics. You're old enough to read the classics. Only real learning counts."

Dan took *War and Peace* from his father's bookcase and read it in five weeks. He talked about Pierre who proved his philosophy by algebra. In each letter Bryan told him to work hard and look after his mother.

Bryan came home on leave and told them he had been posted to India. He tied a knot in the corner of his handkerchief and danced it round the table, like a Rajah with a turban. "It takes more than a World War to get you down," his father said.

"When I die put three hundredweight of marble on my grave, and inscribe it: 'Laugh This One Off', Bryan replied.

At school Dan tried to study, had few friends, rarely wrote home. Each term he won the form prize for Poetry Speaking. He enjoyed standing along on the broadstage, pronouncing the words of poems perfectly, making his voice break with emotion. He received his prize to a patter of clapping.

In the holidays there were air raids. An oil bomb dropped on the park. It seemed more real than other bombs: a tank of oil falling from up there onto the ground. Oil seemed heavier than steel. A morning bomb shattered the bathroom windows, covering the floor with powdery glass. His mother screamed and weeped:

"Your father always shaves at eight o'clock and today he didn't. Thank God. Thank God. There is a God after all!"

Dan helped her sweep up the glass; she held the newspaper while he swept the glass onto it. The monkey vase had got broken, so he went out for some Seccotine.

Where the corner newsagent had been still smelt of charred wood and dusty rubble. He wondered about the paper bill.

At home his mother called from the kitchen: "Mend it in here, Danny, and keep me company. And put some newspaper on the table so the glue won't make so much mess." "It will make the same mess but it won't matter so much," he said.

He popped the monkeys into the vase and said he'd like his Rolls Royce with grey Hooper coachwork. The cat got a piece of paper glued to his fur, and raced round the kitchen chased by the paper. They laughed and she hugged him till he had to push away to breathe, still laughing.

One morning very early he started off to cycle into the country. He heard his mother running after him.

"Wait Danny. I'll walk with you a little way. I'm taking some cheesecake over to Dolly's. Jack's not well."

He called back:

"I must get to Hertford by lunchtime."

But he waited for her, and they went along together, she holding the handlebar while he rocked his feet against the pedals. He wobbled over the road.

"I must get on," he said, impatient.

He heard the hum of a plane.

"Please leave go."

Heavy sound of the plane, throbbing. Gurrumgurrum - gurrumgurrum loudsoft loudsoft loudsoft a heart. He was fifty yards down the street when the noise stopped and the thought flashed "Buzzbomb". Roar and boom into his eyes. The front wheel yanked sideways. He felt his elbow slithering against asphalt. His sleeve filled with blood. He ran to his mother. She lay on her back, stretched out as he had seen her sunbathing in the garden. Only her foot seemed twisted. The weight of that foot on the ground. The brown leather shoe, lace pulled tight and neat, double bow tied precisely. The leather had the glow that comes from unthinking morning polishing over years, brown turning to black with work. The force of the blow against the asphalt road had torn open the outer leather in one place exposing its yellow inside like the slit belly of a pussfilled pig.

A policeman wrote in his notebook: *Scratch on left shoe approx one inch.* The foot had a slight unnatural twist at the ankle. She could not have bent her foot like that if she had been alive. The difference was small, an angle of ten degrees. But alive she could not have done it without breaking the bone, gouging one bone into the other, wrenching the muscle enough to make her scream with pain or come as near to screaming as an ill middle-aged woman can, not a young clean scream, but a choke, a sob, a cough, a constriction in the throat caused by too much trying to escape at one time. Weight is being drawn into the earth, pulled to the middle of it. Her foot weighed.

"She's bought it," the policeman said.

He dragged the body into a doorway beside a butcher's shop. He bawled up a steep flight of stairs:

"Someone give us a 'and?"

A man came downstairs. He unlocked a door into the shop and helped carry the body inside. Dan could see them standing up in the shop, the body between them on the sawdust floor. They took no notice of him. He ran up the stairs and stood on the unfamiliar landing. A door was partly open, and through the E-shaped gap he saw a woman in a yellow electric lit room. She wore a yellow flowered dressing gown. She was kneeling in front of a fireplace, trying to pull the string from a bundle of firewood. It caught on splinters. She poked one stick through, then another, then two or three at a time until the whole bundle collapsed. She threw the sticks on crumpled newspaper. She added small coal to the pile, then put a match to it. She dropped the string on the flames.

He was freewheeling downhill homewards. He had ridden into the country, as far as Hertford. Smoke rose straight from the chimney. Through the windows he saw his father playing chess.

He stood in the dining room, waiting for the solemn talk. He looked at her empty chair, remembered seeing her white bottom once when he'd gone into their bedroom without knocking.

He was taken upstairs to the spare room. He had stationed hundreds of lead soldiers over the floor, flicked marbles at them. An unused bookcase held Bryan's old books, Left Book Club, Thinker's Library. He tried to cry.

"You'd better go back to school. It would be best."

"But it's holidays. There'll be no one there."

"Never mind. We'll ring them up."

From the country railway station he cycled to school: through the village, along a muddy land, bumping down into puddled hollows, watching the marks of tires in thin mud. The camouflaged waterworks crawled with yellow monsters. His head felt queer, like blotting paper. He stopped. He looked up at the flat sky. It was empty except for those specks floating past his eyes which he knew were caused by minute particles slipping between the retina and the iris, and slowly easing down.

That term he missed the big food parcels from home. So he stole from the Food Cupboard: he slid back the brown door just a few inches, pushed his hand inside and picked up whatever was nearest, a bar of chocolate, a tin of sardines.

He was senior enough to have a study. He shared with Michael, a smoothfaced neat boy whose father was a Member of Parliament. Michael was to enter politics.

"I think my first step will be to obtain a position in local government," he told Dan.

"A job with the Council? I wouldn't do that."

"Why?"

"Haven't you seen that notice on their carts? It reads:

"Gratuities Forbidden". I'd like a job where you can make something on the side."

Michael talked about his family, proudly of his father, glowingly of his sister. Dan was invited to Sunday lunch. The father gave him orangeade and remarked that the weather was pretty frightful for cricket. Dan said that today was not good but it was better than yesterday. The day before had been perhaps a little better than yesterday but not quite so good as today. Tomorrow the position would be complicated still further, and the day after that the complexity would become unbearable. Suicide, and an eternity of good (or bad) days, seemed the only solution. Michael got the biggest helpings of roast beef; his sister was tall and wore thick stockings. Over lunch Dan talked about incest and the Oedipus complex.

Michael used the study less often. Dan enjoyed being alone. He ate fingersful of Radio Malt. He looked up words in the dictionary. Rape is an administrative division of Surrey. He began to write an Epic Poem. He borrowed his brother's typewriter. His father sent him a ream of foolscap typing paper. Dan typed on the first sheet, a word: *Onion*. And then, Brilliantly: *Man. Onion Man.* What a picture! Was there another mind in the school that could have conceived it? In the whole county of Gloucestershire, in England, Europe, the Universe? Time was grander. Multiply together all the billions of minds and moments there had ever been: had one once deliberately and self-consciously thought: Onion Man? Pause. Knowledge. How many men there were whose life was onions, whose sons had onion seller owner eater dealer digger Dads. Uniqueness demanded disjointedness. Irrelevance was the key. To Onion add the word least like onion . . .

He was picked for the House chess team and decided to become a professional. His father sent him untidy parcels of books by Lasker and Capablanca and he swotted the first chapters. He played chess with Montague who had been brought up in Chicago and Paris, had a motor bike, girl friends, cigars, colored waistcoats and a thousand gramophone records which he and Dan listened to on sports afternoons. They conversed about composers.

"Of course the move from Beethoven to Brahms reflected the growing complexity of the contradictions inherent in capitalist society," said Dan.

"Say bud, you don't say so!" Montague replied.

"Yearh, Clodface, I do say so."

The music formed a background to Dan's thoughts about himself.

They played word games.

"Describe midsummer in terms of sound," Montague said.

"Beethoven's Ninth performed by an orchestra with ten million first violins and the Massed Choirs of the Universe. And midwinter?"

"The sound made when T. S. Eliot taps his teeth with his spectacles."

They discussed genius. Was Dan a genius?

"You're obsessed with the word," Montague said.

"But what does it mean?"

"Genius is another name for pride," said his friend, "and pride is the cardinal virtue."

"Genius is the ability to achieve extraordinary things," said Dan.

"No, it is the achievement, by work, of extraordinary things. For example, could you spend the entire week at school, saying only 'fish paste'?"

"I am unique and I will amaze people," said Dan.

"Unique? That's very ordinary. And who fails to amaze their mo-father?" his friend asked.

"Aren't you a genius?"

"You mean will I exchange recognition? I'm afraid not. You remain the supplicant."

Soon after he was made a Prefect, Dan walked into Montague's formroom:

"You're making a shocking noise. This is a sixth form and should be an example to the others."

They looked at him, silent. Montague was smiling.
"And don't smile when you are being admonished."

As he left he heard his friend's French-American drawl:
"*Quel sang froid! Quelle savoir faire!*"

The boy bent over correctly and touched his toes. The skin on his bare legs and buttocks stretched tight. He was trembling.
"The other way," Dan said.

The boy straightened a little, touched the edge of the washstand with his hands. He was thirteen. At the daily "hands inspection" he had been caught three times with dirty finger-nails. The traditional punishment was a caning by the Duty Prefect. Dan wanted to thrash him. He was beautiful and Dan wanted to hurt and bruise him. He let the cane touch the boy's skin.
"Get to bed. You're lucky this time."

Dan was reprimanded. He said he could not support capital punishment, no he meant corporal punishment. The dignity of man, Tom Paine, scientific humanism, principles. His Prefect's tie, red with a gold stripe, was formally taken away from him at a special ceremony in the Prefects' Common Room.

"You have precisely one hour left, gentlemen."

The invigilator's plummy voice, artificial as a Bishop's, sounded through the examination hall. Dan's school-leaving certificate, English Literature. The main question read:
"Dr. Johnson was the Hero of his Age. Discuss."

Dan wrote:

Johnson in the Modern Eye

Johnson was god. And typical of his age. Era of Goodsense worship, sameness the ultimate ideal, piggery and prudery rife, nonsense wisdom, pomposity prestige.

So the Nightmareman Must — mountain of conventional revulsion, foul-mannered filth loving big boar beast — of course he Must be part of every mantelpiece. A great lumping tasteless victorian grandfather clock, stumpgomping on top of and right through the pretty coffee cups and sniki simplicities. How he bounds! And Boswell is his weak-tea shadow And the drawing-room clusters and the Dryden Chandelier and the Johnson and the titters are blushed and the boom begins . . . he would not like little cracker nuts but with big lumping joll stump off with blugging beaf hunks. And guzzle. And cover his ear with gravy. And guffaw. And stuck his feet and glush his mouth the modern dainty mind reflects recedes back back

But now when the cooling stonily creeps me and I can see him just plain big, not glumping, clumsy yes but his thud was live and he jollily glowed in thrilling proudness of Town and culture and coffee house fine conversation and rightness (who will read it? of the good occasion and the truth

And he warms his behind by the redfire large and lust and he glows. His great brown pipe I can see in his great brown fist and his boots. Gleaming black and sturdy. The socks must be wool (hand woven quite good) and the lack of a bath quite foul. Thank God I'm here and I'm now away from the stench feast and the big fug   for I'm modern and fine young man.

"Idiot!" Montague said, "they'll fail you."

Dan knew it. He felt sick.

"I won't fail. I don't care if I fail. I'll show them. I won't join the Army. I won't get a job. I won't queue. I'd rather walk. I'll go to London. I'll get a girl and go up West. She'll curve and have a curvy dress. I'll jive with her. I'll sling her round the room. I'll pull her between my legs. She'll be jumping mad. I'll kiss her cheeks. I'll slap her bum till it stings. I'll burn her name on my arm. I'll sleep with her. I'll sleep in the park. I'll get soaked. I'll march. Hope it pours. Hope we get soaked and drenched and drowned. I'll have a long wet crazy beard. I'll slosh through the gutters. I'll smash their windows. I'll yell. I'll knife you. I'm going up West. Coming? We're dead tomorrow."

"I'm not coming." Montague said.

3

Plank from collar to bum. Head back, eyes set, chin in, shoulders back, tummy in, bottom in, legs straight, heels together, feet at an angle of forty-five degrees, thumbs stretched down the seams of the trousers. Cap band polished, best serge pressed and creased to cut, webbing belt and straps tight clean and tough, pack emptied cut square and plywood stiffened, slices of brass set slick as a flicknife, polished to whiteness. Cap, collar, pack, each precisely parallel to concrete slabs beneath the boots. Eye-blinding scintillating brilliant boots.

The cartoon Brigadier treads slowly by, unbelievably moustachioed, inspecting.

"Completed basic training?"

"Sir!"

"Category?"

"Clerk. General Duties. Sir!"

"Enjoying the Army?"

"Sir!"

Behind, walls of dirt. Deadgrey walls, dirt color. Narrow jail windows. The plaster, hard and flaky with age, crumbles: at a touch powdered wall snows on the scrubbed wood floor. Rifles will not be leaned against walls.

Condemned as uninhabitable each year since 1905, Talavera Barracks were most suitable for the accommodation of National Servicemen during basic training.

"Carry on Sergeant-Major."

"D-i-i-i-i-isMiss!"

A thousand men swivel right on the right heel, bring left leg up till thigh is parallel to the ground: crunching crash as a thousand boots slam down.

The men grumbled across the parade ground. They went to the Naafi, queued for tea, strained forward to see the cakes and bacon sandwiches and Irish girls and sausage and mash. The food was served on bakelite plates by girls in sexless overalls.

The Church of England Hall had dusty lampshades and cobwebs on the walls and you were served by old ladies in floral dresses and hairnets and spectacles. On Tuesdays the Naafi had cod and chips and the C of E was empty. As usual the ladies apologised for not having "frying facilities".

"We've applied so often, but there isn't the money today."

Though tonight was cod nith Dan preferred to sit alone in the C of E with *Titbits* and a cup of tea. He had just heard that the Naafi put something in the teat " to make you sleep well".

"I don't like being done good to on the sly," he said.

He worried about his rifle. The bolt was missing. How could it have happened? Bayonet practice tomorrow. Bound to be rifle inspection. And some idiot had kicked his toe-cap on parade. Need a good two hours work to get it right again. They said burning the leather with a hot iron gave a smooth surface that polished up beautifully. It was a gamble. Perhaps it would ruin them. That bolt. "Pull bolt back for inspection of magazine," Had he failed to "ram bolt securely home" so that it had slipped back onto the ground? He left the canteen quickly and ran to the parade ground. He tried to find the spot where his Section had been having rifle instruction. It was dark. He got down on his knees to look. The smoothlooking concrete was rough and jagged to touch. Like a razor blade under a microscope.

"See a pin, pick it up, and all that day you'll be in the bleedin' shit. What the hell are you doing?"

It was Bert.

"Riding a bloody bicycle. I'm looking for my rifle bolt," said Dan.

"Blimey! It shouldn't happen to me ma-in-law. You'll get ten years jankers!"

"That's why I'm looking for it."

"Bet someone nicked it. Well, be 'ung for a bleedin' sheep. Come on to Parsons Field."

"What for?"

"Apples. Lovely red ruddy apples."

Dan didn't want apples.

"Okay I'll come."

In the dark they climbed among fruit trees, pushing apples in to all their pockets. Bert had brought his kitbag and they saw him heaving it on his shoulders, heard a loud whisper: "I'm off."

Ginger, Dan's partner in latrine fatigues, was mooning about in the shadows. Dan was giving him a leg up a tree when a huge hand thudded on his shoulder. He fell back, Ginger on top of him. Sprawling on the ground they saw standing over them a giant with a shotgun.

"Look at that shotgun," whispered Dan, "he can keep his ruddy daughter."

"None o' your lip."

He was enormous. Dan kept quiet. They were taken into a brightly lit kitchen and stood against the wall "to wait for the military". Sergeant Lewis came:

"You'll be up before the C.O. for this."

"Ya yah yah yah yah yah YAAAAAAAAA!" screamed Sergeant Bussel. "That's the way. Yell as you charge. Scare him to death. Hands grip the butt, and UP into his guts. No slashing about the face. UP into his guts. There's no second chances with bayonets. It's him or you. And those Ruskies know a thing or two I can tell you. Right now. First man."

A man ran at the dummy and prodded it with his bayonet.

"Yell!" yelled the Sergeant, "and HATE him! There's no hate in you lads. You don't last long with a bayonet without hating. Next man!"

The dummy on the rope was still moving, and Dan went to steady it before the next man charged. He saw that someone had painted a moustache and spectacles on the face.

Sergeant Bussel shouted like a madman: "What do you think you're doing? Come back here! At the double! Who's in command of this exercise? Who's been running this lot for twenty years? You or me? Who told you to touch the target before the charge? Want to get sliced up? And who'd carry the can back?

"I thought it should be straight, Sergeant."

"Who told you to think? Would Ivan sit 'straight' while you went up nice and polite and stuck a bayonet in his guts?"

"No, Sergeant."

"Right then. Next man. And YELL."

No rifle inspection. There was a God after all.

The bolt wrapped in paper, lay on Dan's bed. On the paper a word: "Thanks". Dan checked the number, rammed it home, sat on the bed, thinking about apples.

"We're on the Board," said Ginger, C.O.'s Office, 1400 hours."

"Christ," Dan said.

Roaring at them, the Regimental Sergeant Major drove them into the Office, marching them in treblequick time. Bareheaded, they stood stiff at attention, rigid. Across the wide desk the Commanding Officer looked up from a file of papers. "Sergeant Lewis?"

"Sir. At 1700 hours I relieved Sgt. Watkins as Orderly Sergeant—."

The C.O. snapped: "Where did you find the accused?"

"Sir. I proceeded to the premises where I found the accused with apples in their possession which they admitted were not their property. Sir."

"Thank you Sergeant. You men, have you anything to say?"

Ginger said: "I didn't know they were private apples sir. I just saw them and nipped over and nicked them. I thought it was all right sir. Everybody—."

"Yes yes. Graveson?"

"I only want to say I am very sorry indeed sir for all the trouble I have caused and—."

"Very well. I have carefully considered the facts of this case .... Far too much disregard for the property rights of neighboring landowners . . . Fine of ten pounds."

"No C.B. and no fatigues!" Dan was laughing. "He couldn't wait to get back to his brandy!"

I'd rather fatigues. It's a ruddy fortune," said Ginger.

"It'll be stopped out of your pay. You'll hardly notice it."

"I already send my mum a pound a week and she keeps saying that's not enough. She thinks I'm made of money."

"A pound a week!"

"I gave her four in civvy street. Now what can I tell her?"

"Write and explain what's happened."

"Tell her there's a thief in the family? She'd never laugh that one off."

"Thief? Still, you can't send her anything for the next ten weeks. Haven't you an uncle who could help?"

Ginger shrugged his shoulders.

"Perhaps I could—?" Dan said.

"Nah."

He walked off, hands in pockets.

Dan wondered how he could pay his own fine. His father's five pounds a month had all gone. He would ask Bryan. He composed a letter. It was difficult. He remembered Bryan's return "after the war". The special troop train. The first glimpse in the crowd of the white shirt, red tie, blue jacket worn by troops in hospital. Bryan had just been re-classified "walking sick". "My biggest thrill in years." The absolute change. Thinning hair, nervous glancing eyes, no concentration. "No wounds, no gallantry in action," he said, "just dreary killing malaria." Bryan sent the ten pounds in a registered envelope, without a message. But the fine was paid, that was the main thing.

Queen's Regulations, War Office Orders, Army Orders, Standing Orders for Division, Regiment, Battalion. These were all transmitted down to Battalion level. Battalion headquarters was neck-deep in Orders. More important, all Orders were continually revised and amended. Important for Dan because he was orders Clerk. He had scissors and paste. He cut out the new revised version, and pasted it over the old. The amendments were specially printed to cover entirely on the page, the paragraph they were intended to replace. Dan was instructed to paste the slivers of paper by their edges, so that they could be lifted up and the old Order consulted, because certain matters remained governed by the old Orders. For example, stores purchases in 1946 would stay governed by the Orders of that year; amendments to the Stores Purchasing Orders therefore must not be allowed completely to obscure the 1946 Orders. Dan became skilled at amending amendments to previously amended Orders. And, like all H.Q. personnel, he was allowed to wear shoes instead of boots and gaiters. He did not have to clean his boots or blanco his gaiters.

He was waving Queen's Regulations over his desk, the latest amendments, flowing paper tails, looped the loop, flapped backwards and forwards. Captain Ames came in, with a young Gunner. The Captain wanted all Forms and Regulations relating to signing on in the Regular Army. "They will be sent to your office, Sir."

"No, better do it now."

The Captain pulled two chairs up to Dan's desk, motioning the Gunner forwards. They sat down, and the boy, hunched over his pen, filled in the forms slowly and carefully. His nails were bitten and dirty. Dan could read the black capitals. *Donald MacAndrew. 18 years.* He looked nearer fifteen, had spots on his chin. *Crane Driver's Assistant. Expresses a desire to join Her Majesty's ... Twelve years engagement.* Typewriters clicked. The boy peered about the office, as if trying to find his way about. The Sergeant nodded and smiled. Captain Ames said: "Jolly good show."

The boy seemed pleased to have pleased everyone. Dan tried to catch his eye but did not manage to do so.

* * *

"Get up, you lazy bastard!" Bert hurled a pillow against the wall above Dan's head, bringing a shower of plaster down on him.

"You're on the Board."

"Not again!"

"It's all right mate, you're going to be a ruddy Officer."

Twelve foot drop. Impossible. Better stay in the ranks for ever. Why did they need an Assault Course with a twelve foot jump to distinguish between Officer Material and the Other Stuff? The Colonel had talked of "modern methods of Officer selection," but this was feudal.

"Hurry along Gentlemen, only thirty-seven seconds to go."

"Gentlemen"! Dan strained for the New World. With a look straight down, he jumped.

The Selection Board psychiatrist dropped his handkerchief on the floor, looked up at Dan, and said:

"Well?"

"Well what?"

"Talk about what I have just done."

Dan talked, very rapidly: "You have just dropped your handkerchief on the floor. It's a queer thing to do, just like that. It's a dirtyish floor, but your handkerchief is fairly clean, so apparently you don't drop it often. It was queer because it was disjointed, it bore or seemed to bear no relation to what had gone before. That is unusual in a human action. The causal relationship between successive actions is usually apparent. Which sounds clever but is in fact a platitude. No, it is profound and also untrue. My confusion results from my avoiding complex subjects like free will and determinism which are the roots of the question. Things drop with varying velocities, depending on their weight. No, the velocity is constant. I think it called G2 but I don't know what G2 is—."

"That will do. You may go now. Thank you."

As Dan went to the door, the psychiatrist callled after him: "What is that propelling pencil doing in your pocket?"

"It is being a propelling pencil."

"Do those white bits, then, mean that you are a proper Officer Cadet?" his father asked for the third time.

"Fully-fledged. And I carry an Officer's stick. If I get through the course I'll be Second Lieutenant Graveson in three months' time."

"Well Dan, I'm proud of you. You've done something at last. That uniform. Doesn't he look smart Bryan?"

Bryan, from his armchair, said: "Thank God someone in this house looks smart. He looks healthy too. Vitamin packed. Killing must be good for you."

"I haven't slaughtered any Japs, like you did."

"I'm sorry. I got it all wrong. It is training to be a killer that is so good for you. Instruction in annihilation stimulates the hormones. Do you suffer from spots or back-ache? Have you got a bad leg? Have three months' fun with a bayonet and feel young again!"

"Just because you took five years to reach a Corporal —."

"That's enough!" their father said. "We're going out to dinner. To celebrate. I've booked a table. So stop quarrelling you two while I go up and shave.

"Doesn't he shave in the morning any more?" asked Dan, when he had gone.

"It's Saturday," said Bryan.

But he would not let go.

"Yes, we're proud of you Dan. We'll sit at home in the next war, being blown to atomic smithereens happy in the knowledge that you're at the Front winning glory!"

"You were mighty glad of the Atom Bomb when it stopped the war and brought you home."

Bryan stoop up.

"Glad? You bloody fool! You sodding bloody little baby!"

"I'm sorry."

"Perhaps I was just nearer to it than you were. But since that Bomb I've felt like I had Leprosy, like bits of me were dropping off."

"It brought you home," Dan insisted.

"Half-dead."

Dan said: "You used to be a scientific humanist."

"Labels going cheap! Scientific what? Tell it to the Japs. They're still dying from an overdose of science. Have you heard the latest from the States? They say a cure for radiation sickness is theoretically possible. Spread the glad news in Hiroshima and Nagasaki. Scientists may even now be tackling the theoretical problem of raising the one hundred and twenty-eight thousand Japanese dead."

"It's not the scientists, it's war, and the causes of war —."

"General Graveson begins to think! Who ordered you to think?"

Their father came in, in his dressing-gown, soap frothing his face. A white blob fell on the carpet.

"You'll wear your uniform Dan?"

"Of course. I'll have to press it though. Have you got an iron?"

Bryan said: "In the kitchen, by the bread bin. Sorry Dad, I can't come tonight, I don't feel so good. Got the shivers. Perhaps I'll join you later for a drink."

"Please come," Dan said, "I want you to."

"Some other time. Sorry.

Dan went to press his uniform, his father to finish shaving. Bryan watched the soap bubbles sink into the carpet.

Gilt and green nudes danced among flowers round the walls. Tablecloths and waiters' shirtfronts glistened in the artificial gloom.

"It's very smart. Costs a fortune. But you don't get made an Officer every day," his father said.

"I've told you so many times. I've got a three month's course to get through yet.'

"You'll do it. You can get anything you really try for. I've always said you were the clever one."

"No. Bryan is."

"Why don't you two get on these days? You used to."

"He's so ratty. He blows up over nothing."

"You must give him time to settle down," his father said. "I'm worried about him. He never sees anybody or wants to do anything. He doesn't sleep, just walks about all night — we meet in the kitchen at two in the morning and eat cornflakes! If only he had some friends, especially a girl friend. He needs one. Any man does."

"I suppose so."

Waiters handed them each a huge Menu.

"Have anything you like, Dan. Have the best. Do you like smoked salmon? And there's a whole capon cooked in wine, with asparagus or mushrooms."

"I want something extraordinary and rare that I've never had before."

His father ordered oysters, Lobster Newbourg, Boeuf Stroganoff. He studied the Wine List.

"We'll have a good claret, Leoville Lascases '28. You'll have to learn about these things now, Dan."

There was a Cabaret. A fat little man played a grand piano. He composed medleys from popular songs shouted at him by the diners. "Smoke Gets In Your Eyes," shouted his father. "That's a grand old one. Your mother's favorite."

A girl sang. The lights went low and she danced, chased by a white spotlight. Her shiny dress fell in a heap on the floor. Two chorus girls joined her, hiding her with long fluffy fans. She held a fan herself and moved around followed by the two girls. For seconds at a time Dan could see the girl's white-lit nude body as the fans hesitated. It was intentional. He glanced at his father.

"Have a liqueur, Dan. For Officers only. Green Chartreuse," 'I'm sozzled."

"There's someone I would like you to meet, Dan."

"As long as it's not Auntie Lulu. I can't stand Auntie Lulu."

"I haven't seen Lulu for a long time. We've been very alone, your brother and I."

"I know."

"It's been too much. But you could help, Dan, if you wanted to."

"Me help you? That's a new one!"

"We'll see. Let's go now."

They drove through the West End. Dan sat in front next to his father. He felt warm and sleepy. The car pulled up outside a block of flats.

"Let's have a goodnight drink, Dan. And you can meet Helen."

In the self-operated lift there were six black studs with clear silver numbers. His father pressed "3".

"Darling! What a lovely surprise!" she said.

She was thin. Red hair. Young.

"And I know who this is. Come in Daniel. Let me take your coat. What will you have?"

"Nothing thanks, had too much already."

"Don't be silly, have a small gin."

I'm not silly. No thanks."

His father said: "Helen's only trying to —."

"I know that. It's very nice of you. But I just couldn't take a drop more. Specially as I think I'll have to drive Dad home!"

"We'll have coffee," she said, "I'll put the kettle on."

Dan sat in one deep armchair, and his father sat in another. "It's a lovely room." Dan said.

"Yes. Dan, I've known Helen for some time. She's been wonderful to me. I know you'll get on well with her."

"Of course I will."

She poured the coffee:

"It's a wonderful machine, darling, it doesn't clog up like the French one."

"I thought the chromium sieve-plate would be an improvement."

"It makes very good coffee," said Dan.

She uncrossed her legs and got up to pour Dan a second cup. She leaned over him.

"My, you look swell in that uniform."

"Thank you. And that's a very nice dress."

His father smiled.

"I'll take them in," Dan said.

He collected the coffee cups, put them on the tray, carried them into the kitchen. He washed them under the tap and placed them on the stainless steel draining-board. He looked for a drying-up cloth. He went back to the room to ask Helen. They were standing up and kissing hard in the well-lit centre of the room.

"I'm sorry."

"Come and kiss Helen goodnight, Dan," his father said quite loudly.

"No."

Dan could see he was holding her hand very tightly.

His father said: "Well we've had our goodnight kiss. So it's time to go."

Dan picked up his Army greatcoat from the back of a chair. 'You stay. I can easily get home by tube. It's a direct line, no changes."

He had one arm through his coat-sleeve.

"Don't be silly," his father said.

"Seems to be my silly night."

He was feeling vaguely for the other arm-hole.

They drove home together, with the car radio playing dance music.

He blobbed out the first big triangle. Two triangles left, eight oblongs, fifty-six circles. An infantry officer must excel the best of his men in anything he may order them to do. Assault course, route march, musketry, manoeuvres, rope-climbing, weapon-training, swimming, fencing, rugger, drill. Drill. No time to think? It is intentional, you are going to be an officer not a philosopher. Lectures on tactics, man-management, venereal diseases, regimental history, Russia, Korea, Malaya, mess—etiquette, signals, strategy, leadership. Cadets when dressed in civilian clothes will wear trilby hats. Cadets will not engage in conversation with Other Ranks. Dan stumbled from day to day, counting the days. On Sundays after Church Parade, when he walked in the town he wore his officer-type raincoat, carried his officer's cane and once or twice was saluted by young national servicemen.

He didn't care that he was an officer.

"Congratulations! Of course you'll be coming home for your leave," his father wrote. It seemed Bryan was shamming ill again, sitting in a deckchair in the garden, staring, or lying in bed all day. The idea clearly was for Dan to sit with him, spend his leave playing chess, reading Proust aloud, making coffee, being polite to Helen, chatting, visiting relations in his new uniform. No. He was going to have a good time.

He drew his first month's officer's pay, wrote home to say that he had already arranged a holiday "with some newly-commissioned Officer friends". And by the way he would not need the five pounds a month any more, thanks for sending it so regularly.

He packed a bag and alone in a taxi went to the railway station.

"Single to Llangollen, please."

He loved the sound of the name, that was why he had chosen it.

He booked a room at a hotel. A steamy hot day. He walked in the park, searching. He knew he didn't care what she was like as long as he could have her without you or anyone or her knowing.

A girl lay on the grass in front of him. Her hair spread a pool of blond on the green. Her body spreadeagled, arms and legs wide, cheek against the warm lawn. The earth curved against her tummy and thighs and breasts. He felt the weight of heat in the leaves. Minute eyes of birds winked. A slow plane murmured by. She raised herself so he could see into her blouse. Her breasts moved with her breathing: lowering to brush the ground then rising barely to touch it. A grasshopper, conspicuous on the smooth lawn, was jumping away to shelter. He caught it gently: pale green, dark green, streaks of hazel brown. He took it to her.

"Look at this."

"He's lovely," soft Welsh voice, "let him go now."

She pulled his fingers apart and the insect hopped out and away.

"Did you hear about the pea-catcher? he asked.

"Tell me."

"A man stood on a high flat roof, threw a pea up, took a step back and caught it in his mouth, threw a pea up, took a step back and caught it in his mouth, threw a pea up, took a step back, fell a thousand feet, feet first. It's an old Welsh folk-tale taught me by my Granny."

"No."

"No. I made it up."

"I can see you talk a lot."

"Too much."

His hand played with her heavy fair hair, slid inside her blouse, held her breast, squeezed till his nails bit deep, felt the nipple rise hard in his palm. He strayed, searching and feeling, beneath her wide shirt.

"Let's go over there, to the trees," she said.

They walked easy together, arms round waists, to the shadow of the trees. He stretched beside her, moved closer, lay over her, in.

"I love you." he said.

"You say that easily."

"Can you make love without loving?"

"Don't be silly, of course I love you. I saw you come into the park, wandering round, and I thought you were lovely."

"What's your name?"

"Deirdre Watkins. I work in a shop. But I'm studying fashions, to be a designer."

"I'm Lieutenant Daniel Graveson — just call me Dan."

"My brother's in the army," she said, "I thought you were something like that."

They lay close, without talking.

She said: "Have you seen our swans?"

She took him to see the lake, over the other side of the park. They watched the swans floating slowly, careful, deceiving. He was dizzy with them, felt their softwhiteness. Two swans together suddenly whizzed off the water skinning the surface with their feet, like waterskiers. They fluttered heavily around, realised the air was not for them, came skidding down, bottoms first. Ducks bounced on the small waves.

An alien starched Scottish Nanny sat on the bench beside them, lecturing her neat child:

"It's fesh not wishes, fesh not wishes. It's time you were learning to say the few words you do say, properly. Do you want a sweet?"

"No."

"Thank you."

"Fank you."

A moment later: "Nanny, can I have a sweet?"

"Please."

"Pease."

Across the lake a herd of mauve and white schoolgirls giggled and yelped, like flamingos drinking the Amazon. An intermittent "peep" came from an angry schoolteacher blowing her whistle, the toneless cry of an unimaginative bird.

A brilliant scarlet speed boat went mad in the middle of the lake, whinning round in small circles. A big boy in a striped blazer told them:

"It's got enough petrol to keep that up for three days."

"Hurrah!" Dan said.

"We'd better be going, Dan, there's a storm coming."

They hurried back the way they had come. They reached the trees just in time. Came a maniac intensity of the sun; the shadowed side of sunlit leaves showed black, veinless. Pearly pregnant evening light invaded the afternoon. Rain fell grey against blueblack trees. They moved to where the trees were so thick that the sunlight was always shut out: no grass, only bare earth under layers of dead leaves. They were safe and dry. They looked out. A huge weight of rain drove like iron across the park, soaking drenching flooding, making the lawns wallow in water, forcing water into the flowerbeds, compelling the flowers to gulp and swallow hundredweights of water.

It drizzled. Raindrops filed along twigs. Budge up. Budge up. Drops, dropped from leaf to leaf to ground. "While it's pouring it's driest under the trees, but afterwards it's wettest." she said.

It stopped. The last waters sluiced away. The air was clear.

A Police car zizzed past them, microphone bellowing. Among the incomprehensible syllables Dan heard "Graveson." Impossible. The car was away and turned a corner. A grave young policeman walked on the other side of the rainshining street, impregnable in helmet, cape, waterproof boots. Dan told her about his brother's mock-German:

"LuftwaffenBomben, Watford-By-Pass gebomben, Auntie Dolly gebomben, Ark Royal ein zwei drei gebomben, Corporal Graveson gebomben, Schikelgruber uber alles gebomben. . . . ."

They held hands past the hotel receptionist. In the corridor he joked:

"Do you come here often?"

"Of course not. Do you think I'm that kind of girl?"

"At least you've heard about "that kind of girl". I didn't know they had them in Llangollen."

"If you don't stop I'm going straight home."

"Only kidding."

Arm round her waist, hand on the door-knob, he kissed her.

On the carpet, just by the door (it had been pushed under the door) lay a telegram.

NO.

"Your brother."

His fist was through the wardrobe; the mirror inside was shattered. He waved his fist about so that it bled all over the fawn carpet spattering it with purplish stains.

The girl stood still, one hand white on the mock-walnut dressing-table, looking at the stains. She packed his things into his bag, went downstairs to explain to the manager.

"He was very understanding," she said.

She handed him his bag.

"I'll never see you again."

He didn't say anything.

He could not decide whether to walk to the station or get a taxi. It was not far, yet the bag was heavy. Platform one. Which platform? Platform one.

Early morning. He fumbled at the burglarproof doublelock. Helen opened the door.

"Hello Dan. Glad you could come so quickly. Your father is upstairs.

The house was ordinary. The dead body had been taken to hospital to make sure it was dead. He opened the door of their room. His father was sitting up in bed, backed by pillows, reading the *Daily Mail.* Dan said nothing because he could not think of anything to say.

Doors of expensive cars slammed heavy. Husbands waited while wives tittivated. Thicker greyer overcoats from Leeds greeted slick tight London ones. Stretched-and-skinny car reflections had squeezed waists, bodies split into two shrinking pears, or tears. Ladies' sharp high heels spiked between the new grey gravel stones, men trod the gravel down. Stone cemetery arch, square cemetery building of stone. Foreign, clean, preserved from contact with the countryside. Chemical sprays and regular scrubbing with disinfectant killed small creepers and scraps of moss. Not a fleck of grass, not a living insect survived to spoil the stone. They filed in, past a pile of broken prayerbooks heaped on a backless chair. They edged round the walls, chatted hushedly, continually. No coffin, only an oblong space of floor. Outside, somewhere, the body lay in its warm brown varnished box.

"Move in a little closer if you please thank you," the priest said. Like a market salesman to his customers. Were they the customers, or was the thing in the box? If depended whether the funeral expenses were charged to the deceased's estate, or were paid by the surviving relatives. Dearly beloved. The priest was enjoying his rich voice. Cut off in his prime. Splendid young man. Loyal son and brother. Credit to his church. Brilliant mind and wonderful promise. Mourned by all who remember his loving nature. Dust unto dust. Recitative without end. He towed them down the long path to the yellow trench to watch the coffin dumped in. The body in the sheet in the coffin in the earth was in the universe.

"Unassuming, Unpretending,
Straight the Path of Life he trod,
May his Bliss be never ending
Thro' the Mercies of his God."

Oh God.

4

Brother officers gathered round him.

"Fighting for freedom and democracy with the Yanks in Korea? You can't believe that rubbish!" Dan was saying.

"Another whisky?" Lieutenant Crabbe stooped over the siphon; hard head, thick ginger stubble. He had a parachute badge, and medals.

"Here's a stiff one. Or would you prefer vodka?"

"Thanks. Remember Hiroshima. A hundred and twenty-eight thousand bodies. What colossal contempt they must feel for us with our measly machine guns."

"You mentioned that before."

"Then tell me, who profits from the war? Korea? China? The answer may show who started it."

Someone said: "Those yankee millionaires you were talking about, with their arms factories —."

"Yes," said Dan, "and there were five million American unemployed before the arms drive solved that problem overnight. There's no unemployment or arms manufacturers in the New China."

"They produce a deal of arms."

"But not privately," Dan said.

"Does that make any difference?"

"It's a long story. And I must get to bed. I'm drunk."

"Wait a bit," Crabbe said, "so the North Koreans are fighting for peace and independence? Is that right? Let's get the whole thing perfectly clear."

"That's an over-simplification. . .but I can't think straight. I must owe you all buckets of whisky."

"Think nothing of it. It's been a pleasure."

Lieutenant Gerson, an attached Officer from the Education Corps, spoke for the first time:

"Let's talk about something else for heaven's sake."

"Hey, don't spoil the fun," Crabbe said.

Dan blinked.

"Fun?"

He walked over to the mantelpiece, stood with his back to them. Eleven sharp tings sang from the glasscased clock. He knew they had followed him across the room. He watched the moving parts inside the clock swinging and linking, teeth biting precisely into delicate revolving cylinders. He heard the scrape of windows being fastened. He looked down at his reflection in the polished silver tray on which letters addressed to officers were laid. He turned round. They had formed a halfcircle close to him.

"I must get back," he said quietly, "I've some reading to do." (Lenin on Imperialist War; not one of them had read a book like that.)

"Don't go yet, it's been so interesting listening to you. Quite an education."

He wondered where his hat was, he couldn't leave without it, had to have it for parade in the morning. He moved towards the door. A Major stood in front, his tummy stuck out. Dan half saw a brown boot flick out, felt his ankle crack. He put his hands out as he fell, felt the carpet slide against his palms. A hand of iron grabbed his wrist, another twisted back his arm. Crabbe knelt down and spoke to him:

"Now look here, we don't want to break up the Mess. Will you come out like a man?"

"What's happening?. . . .Yes."

He was bundled outside in the middle of eight or nine of them. The cold foggy air hit him. They marched him along a gravel path, then onto grass.

"What good will this do? There's problems to solve, but this is not the way."

"Christ, he never stops."

He thought God what are they going to do to me. I can't speak to them. No way of getting at them. He slithered his heels against the ground. They pushed and punched him along.

They were behind the cookhouse among smelly piles of rubbish and open dustbins. They stopped and held him. Two of them levered up the cast iron cover to the grease pit. Stink came up. They shoved him in. He managed to hold his body above the slime, there was only the smell. Then a hand at the back of his neck pushed his face into the grease, held it there.

He was out, spluttering, yelling after them: "Fascists! Fascists!"

They'd gone. He sicked up onto the grass.

He arrived at breakfast very late next morning, after all the junior officers had gone. A Major and a Colonel sat at one end of the long oak dining table. He sat on his own. On his way out he picked up an envelope from the silver tray, and read, on a piece of cheap lined paper:

"Meet me for coffee at Lyons, 7:30 p.m. this evening. Gerson."

Lyons was crowded. Everyone seemed old or middle-aged. He could not see Gerson. He queued up, bought two cups of tea, sat next to any old grey man who was excitedly reckoning figures down the side of a newspaper. Dan poured sugar into his tea aiming the stream to burst the bubbles round the side of his cup.

Gerson came in, sat opposite, saying:

"Glad you could make it."

Dan looked straight at the eyes pale behind steelrimmed spectacles, pale lips, thin fair hair. Gerson asked the waitress, an old African woman, to bring him a packet of cigarettes.

Dan said: "What do you want to see me about?"

"I want to have a talk with you."

"Hullo."

"Seriously. I want to know what you are trying to do."

"What do you mean?"

Dan was annoyed to see Gerson continually glancing around the room. A nervous habit.

"All this revolutionary talk," Gerson said. "Red Flag wagging like a ten year old."

"I have certain principles —."

"Why not keep them to yourself?"

"It's those Captains and Majors. I want to kick their teeth in.

"You are in a bad way. Don't you know they're laughing at you?"

"I don't care."

"Yes you do, you're not so stupid. I don't know what your job is or what you're trying to do. Frankly I don't trust you enough to tell you anything M.I.5. don't already know. I've been fifteen years in the Party, too long to take chances. But if your care about Peace, and want to do something effective —."

"What could we do?" Dan asked.

"Make a demonstration, a gesture. Have you ever gone chalking?"

"Slogans on walls? No. But that's brilliant. Let's cover the camp with hammers and sickles."

The old man on Dan's left looked up, interested.

109

Gerson smiled: "Lucky we live in England. Tell me, what is the main political task here today?"

"Peace —."

"Right. The reaction to hammers and sickles would be 'help! Russian spies!' Would that tend towards peace or war?"

"The symbol of workers and peasants —."

Gerson interrupted: "Have you seen many peasants lately?"

"Thousands."

"Being peasantless," said Gerson, "is a British peculiarity of great political significance. But that's another matter."

"Then what shall we do? Let's decide now."

"No, I must go. Think about it. But for Christ's sake keep your mouth shut. If you must talk, talk to the men, that way you may learn something. Go down to their lines, or to the Public bars, even the Education Centre. Get to know them. You'll find one or two good ones."

Dan sat looking at Gerson's tea cup. A pale brown skin had formed on the untouched tea. The waitress asked:

"You want this sir?"

"No, thank you very much indeed."

He put the cup with the cups, and the saucer on the pile of saucers on her tray. He looked at her tea-stained overall, the blue cotton skirt with yellow flowers peeping beneath it, thin liquorice legs. How could those skinny ankles bear her weight, hold up that huge bottom? How steeply under her skirt those legs must swell out into giant thighs. She should be sitting in a rocking chair surrounded by grandchildren. Gerson had not said thank you for the cigarettes.

Standing in the Officers' Latrine, a week later, they decided to paint on the Ammunition Store: *Join the Movement For Peace*. It was, in Gerson's phrase, "the correct slogan". Dan thought it was too long.

Gerson said: "It can't be helped. Those words are essential. There may be another comrade along to help us."

"Another comrade"! Dan felt he had been knighted.

Hidden by a rolling heavy midnight fog, Dan waited just outside the camp. He felt safe in the fog and darkness. Gerson loomed up, nosing around looking for him. Dan skipped round behind him, pushed a stick in his back and roared:

"Welcome Comrade!"

"For Christ's sake have some sense." Gerson snapped.

"Can't you take a joke?"

"Yes. Where's the brush?"

"You were bringing it."

"Hell. Now what can we do? We can't paint with our bare hands."

"I'll find something." Dan said.

He ran off and returned twenty minutes later, bearing like an Olympic flame, his shaving brush.

"The best I could find. All the paint brush shops are shut. It's a capitalist conspiracy."

"Watch out for sentries." Gerson said, "you know what happens if we're caught."

They crept across the battalion football field, then through lines of elephantoid field guns.

"Down!"

Dan flopped on the squelchy earth. Ten yards ahead a sentry stood, heavy like a lead soldier, staring. His slung rifle poked awkwardly out of his khaki cape. Gerson, crawling correctly as he had been taught in basic training, moved away, quick and quiet. Dan crawled after, feeling ridiculous.

They reached the ammunition store. Gerson unwrapped a paint tin.

"Take it," he said, "you paint first and I'll keep watch. A short whistle means danger."

He folded and pocketed the brown paper.

"It's oil paint I'm afraid, which is tricky because it stains your clothes. Be careful."

The hut was built of corrugated iron sheets. It had once been painted light green. In places the paint had come away showing rusty orange beneath, elsewhere it bubbled up in wide blisters or formed a separate corrugated skin of thin green. Dan scrubbed the paint on. Green specks and slivers mixed with dollops of white showered over him. The letters began huge and got smaller and smaller as he tired. He did the final "E" and went back to Gerson. But Gerson had gone. He returned to the wall and with the last of the paint added an exclamation mark. The hairs of the brush were rubbed away, only the small bone handle remained.

Huts and guns and piles of junk, grey animals, jumped from the fog, lurched at him. He found he was swinging the paint tin; Gerson had not said how to get rid of it. He passed an empty oil drum which had been stood straight and painted shiny black for a General's inspection. He lifted the edge and pushed the tin inside.

In his room Dan tried to get the oil paint off his hands and uniform. He used paraffin from a lamp kept "For Emergencies".

As soon as he woke he longed to go and see the slogan, but Gerson had forbidden it. He waited by the Naafi, hoping to overhear excited conversation; he was disappointed. However, on the Regimental Notice Board a paper had been pasted over the "afternoon programme". It read:

Important. All ranks will attend parade. Regimental Parade Ground. 1430 hours. A. Digby-Smith. Adjutant.

Dan thought of going sock, or deserting. He could not find Gerson.

He marched at the head of his Platoon, hearing the crunch of their boots on the concrete. His Battalion formed up. The high bawl of the Sergeant-Major.

"Talyar-r-r-n, Talyarr-r-r-n, Shun!"

The Adjutant walked slowly up and down the ranks. Dan held his breath, stared straight ahead. The Adjutant came right up to him, stood glaring, inches away.

"Stand easy, Graveson. Now, let's have a look at your chaps."

Dan relaxed.

"Just a security check," the Adjutant murmured.

"Now men," he turned to them, "each Section in turn will come smartly to attention and all ranks will hold their hands smartly in front of them."

As each man begged for alms, the Adjutant walked gravely by, accompanied by Lt. Graveson. With the tips of his fingers he turned over each pair of hands, and looked at them keenly. A man with big grimy hands and dirty bitten nails, said:

"I work down the boilers, sir."

"Hold your tongue man! Don't you know you're on parade? Speak when you're spoken to!"

The Adjutant looked up at the man, who was a foot taller, and snapped:

"A disgraceful turnout. No excuse. Take that man's name Mr. Graveson."

He smiled at the Sergeant and glanced at his hands too.

"Carry on Mr. Graveson!"

"Yessir! Platoo-oo-oon, by the right, qu-i-i-i-i-ck March!"

Since 1747 Friday had been Regimental Mess Night. From seven o'clock until nine all Junior Officers stood about the Mess Lounge in dress uniform, drinking, chatting, waiting for the C.O. to Lead the Regiment into Dinner. Dan stood fingering the stem on his glass. He heard Gerson's clear clipped voice:

". . . Hunt Ball on Tuesday."

"Where the devil is one to procure scarlet tails these days?" Crabbe asked.

Dan stood near them.

"That's a problem for your regulars," said Gerson, "I think I'll trot along in my D.J."

A pause. They sipped whisky.

"So you're a National Serviceman," Crabbe said, "What were you in before?"

"I'm a lawyer," Gerson replied.

"Defending swindlers and murderers eh?"

"Not exactly. I dealt mainly with land law and property."

"Oh yes."

Crabbe finished his drink.

"What'll you have?" Crabbe asked Gerson.

Dan stood quiet.

"And you old chap?" Crabbe turned to him.

"No thanks," Dan said.

Crabbe brought back two whiskies. On the way he had been thinking.

"What is land law exactly? Sounds a bore,"

"Strangely enough land law is ninety per cent of the law, although less than a tenth of the people own land."

"Why is that?" Dan asked innocently.

"Because most of our laws were made by nineteeth-century landed gentry whose first concern was with their own property."

Crabbe left them. Dan said to Gerson:

"Next week he'll be telling the Mess that land law is ninety per cent of the law and what are they going to do about it."

"Really?" Gerson said, "Please excuse me a moment."

Dan rolled the stem of his glass between his fingers. The chat rose and fell around him. He lit a cigarette.

At a quarter to nine something unusual happened. The Adjutant stood at one end of the lounge banging the table with his glass, calling:

"Quiet Gentlemen. One moment please Gentlemen. Quiet."

There was some whipering. The Adj had drunk only two gins the whole evening, a sign something was brewing.

"I do apologize gentlemen. But the Security chaps have a thing on their mind. And you know what that means. We'll just have to play along with them. This afternoon we had a special parade and inspection for all non-commissioned ranks. Now Intelligence is so dammed thorough, suppose we should thank heavens for it, it seems it will be necessary for us in the Mess to undergo a similar check. A mere formality for completeness, you understand gentlemen. All junior officers then, if you please gentlemen, form along the wall, and we can finish in five minutes."

A roar of voices all talking at once, some protesting, some making jokes, all asking what it was all about. Rapidly the Adjutant walked past glancing at their hands held out. He made it clear that it was not his idea, but that he was formally carrying out superior orders. Dan remembered the early morning spent scrubbing his hands almost raw with pumice stone and scalding water. By electric light the steaks of white across his hands barely showed. The Adjutant checked and passed him without a sign. Perhaps he lingered a moment Dan could not be sure.

A week had passed. The slogan had been blacked over by Military Police before more than a dozen men had seen it. No one quite understood it; there had been some puzzled talk, a paragraph in the *Movement for Peace Newsletter* under "News from the Branches."

"How's it going old boy?"

The Adjutant's hand rested on Dan's shoulder. This treatment was reserved for Field Officers and RSM'S.

"Quite well thank you sir."

"Could you take ten minutes off this afternoon? The C.O. would like a word with you."

"Yes sir. What time would be convenient sir?"

"What about 1430 hours?"

"Well I'm down for firing practice then sir."

The Adjutant frowned.

"Never mind about that Graveson."

"Very well sir."

Rarely did the Commanding Officer talk officially with a person of inferior rank, without being supported by his menials: Second in Command, Adjutant, Regimental Sergeant Major, Aide de Camp. Dan was relieved therefore to find Colonel York quite alone.

"Glad to see you Graveson."

The Colonel did not get up from his heavy leather chair. He sat like an old lion, with whiskery brows, paws for hands, and a way of turning his head round slowly.

"Do sit down. Smoke?"

114

"No thank you sir."

"Wise man."

Dan sat straight on his wooden chair, his hands on his lap. The Colonel glanced down at a file of papers and a copy of Queens Regulations. He pulled at the lobe of his ear, flicked the bristles of his moustache. Dan had seen him behave like this when talking with very senior officers.

"It's about this security report, Graveson. It seems that on the afternoon 3rd July, that is Monday last, during the delivery of a lecture to "P" Company, you were guilty of conduct which amounted to incitement to mutiny. What have you to say?"

"I have absolutely no idea what it is all about sir. There must be some mistake."

"I don't think so." the Colonel murmured. "You were giving instruction on the twenty-five pounders?"

"That is possible."

"You initiated a discussion on the value of the weapon?"

"I prefaced my lecture with a general description of the gun, including its cash cost. I had obtained the information from Regimental Office."

"Indeed. What followed?"

"I'm not sure sir."

"Come come Graveson. I have the details here. But I prefer to know your side of the picture. "Audi alteram partem" you know."

"Well sir, the figures in thousands of pounds meant nothing to the men. So I may have translated them into terms they could understand. One gun equals twenty motor cars, for example."

"Or so many council houses or hospital beds? Did you even find it necessary to discuss the position of old age pensioners?"

"No sir, that was one of the men."

"Did you not ask the men to 'vote' on which they would 'prefer to have their money spent on'?"

"It was not quite like that sir."

"You understand, Graveson, that I cannot have one of my officers carrying on like this."

"Sir."

"No one sympathizes with the pensioners more than I do, but this kind of talk, in the Regiment's time, it's sheer pacifism. Or worse. You join the Army to do a job. A job for your country. If you would prefer to be on the side, very well then. But you cannot have it both ways."

"It seems to me —."

115

"Don't argue with me. And don't interrupt. The fact is Graveson, I am instructed to request you to resign your commission with effect from the 1st of next month. You will have twelve days leave until that date."

"It's a terrible shock sir."

"I'm sorry Graveson. I've never had a thing like this in my Regiment. I cannot concern myself with personal feelings. It's more than a question of regimental discipline, the matter is out of my hands."

"I must have time to think about it."

"That is impossible. I formally request you to resign."

Dan stood up.

"I cannot do that, sir. I consider I have the right of any citizen to hold political views and express them, so long as I do not break army or civil law. If I am charged with an offense, then I wish to be tried by Court Martial. The publicity will no doubt create —."

"You may take whatever action you think fit," the Colonel said decisively. " But I must warn you that a number of other matters, including a recent occurrence you no doubt have in mind, would certainly be raised against you in the event of your acting foolishly. A court martial needless to say has the power to award the heaviest penalties. I still hope we may settle this matter man to man without unpleasantness."

"I am only asking for my democratic —."

"Yes yes yes. Very well, that will be all Graveson. I advise you to consider your position carefully."

"I will sir. Thank you sir."

In the outer office, the Adjutant handed him a typed document:

". . .commanded by Her Majesty to inform you that, following certain admissions, the Army Council have decided that Lieutenant Daniel Graveson should be called upon to . . . .resign his Commission. . . .Should he neglect or refuse to submit his application to resign within fourteen days . . . . steps will be taken with a view to terminating the said Commission with effect from. . ."

"Will you sign for it, sir?" the clerk said.

"What?"

"To show you received it, sir."

"No."

The clerk looked towards the Adjutant, who said:

"Never mind about that now."

He marched smartly across the parade ground among the drilling squads and companies. Orders of command whined and roared over his head. He tried to appear as if he had important business to attend to. But he did not know where to go. A Sergeant glanced at him sideways: did he know? How long would the news take to travel round the camp?

He found himself at the Education Center. Forlorn and empty. Dusty posters told stories in pictures about first aid, fire drill, artificial respiration. Men with moustaches demonstrated life-saving. Old colored maps showed the distribution of barley, wheat and sugar beet in the neighboring fields. Who cared? A film of dust covered the globe's northern hemisphere. The Center was mainly used as a source of drawing-pins. The bottom pins from all the posters had been borrowed, leaving pin-holes and blobs of rust in the flapping corners. Old Major Caulfield came in:

"What can I do for you, Graveson?"

"I'm waiting for Mr. Gerson, if that's all right sir."

"By all means."

Dan watched the sagging face, the huge dark veins in the hands.

"Did I ever show you these, Graveson?"

Glossy photographs of a chubby bouncing man.

"I was Army breast-stroke champion in those days, nineteen-thirty-two."

He still wore his Army Swimming Club blazer and tie. Gerson came in. A spot in the palm of the Major's hand was then travelling towards his heart, a thickening, a slight thickening of the blood, easing towards the muscular heart to cover over and close two hefty pounding vital bloodfilled arteries and stop the flow of blood. He'd be gone, and turned to slime.

"The granting of a commission," said Gerson, "is part of the Queen's prerogative. There need be no court martial, no appeal. That which Her Majesty giveth, she may also take away. But you can make a political fight. Do you want to?"

"I'll do anything."

"Don't underate the strenght of the forces against you. Don't start a battle you can't win. Will your own platoon speak up for you? Can you depend on any of the NCO's, or your brother officers? What about your family?"

"I don't expect much help from anyone else."

"I see. Well how do you propose to start the campaign?"

"I am prepared to follow out any plan the Communist Party proposes."

Gerson said nothing for a minute, then: "In my opinion you should resign with as little fuss as possible."

* * *

"Dan! We're going to Helen's. Put your uniform on," his father called up the stairs.

"I'm sick to death of the bloody uniform."

"Do as you please."

Then, on the last day of his leave, a letter arrived, addressed to "265546221 Pte. Graveson, D". His father held it out to him: "What's all that about?"

Dan read the short printed letter.

"Good news. I've been posted to another unit. It's quite close by, Epping Forest. On the Central Line. I'll be able to get home for the weekends."

"Aren't you an Officer any more?"

"The envelope? That's just a typist's error."

In the car, outside the tube station, his father said.

"You're in some trouble."

"It's nothing."

"Then why the long face? I'm a bit older than you —."

"Old enough to be my father."

"And I still know a thing or two. If only you'll tell me what kind of a jam you're in —."

"Raspberry. I've been demoted, temporarily."

"I knew it. What happened?"

"Well the C.O. is an absolute tyrant. Real Guards disciplinarian. Punishment parades for the slightest mistake. He's completely inhuman. I lead a deputation of the men to complain, I threatened we'd see our M.P's and get publicity in the papers. . . .It was nearly a mutiny."

"What about your Communist friend, whatsisname, Gherkin?"

"He thinks I did a good job."

"But he's leading the trooops from behind?"

"No. In the developing political situation —."

"I don't give two pins for the blasted situation. He got you into this mess, can he get you out?"

"The Government is tottering —."

"And a puff of your adolescent emotion is going to bring the Government down! You've been cashiered and ruined your career and you still shout *Daily Worker* slogans at me."

"You're doing the shouting, Dad."

"You'll miss your train. Better go now. I was going to tell you: I've been trying to get you into the Inns of Court, to read for the Bar. I only hope they don't ask me for your Army record."

They went into the station. His father bought the ticket, handed it to him, with a five pound note.

"You'll be needing this now, Dan."

"Thanks."

"Don't thank me, keep out of trouble. And you'll find a law book in your bag. No harm in a bit of swotting if you get the chance."

"I will. Thanks for everything. Give my love to Helen. Cheerio Dad."

"Goodbye."

Alone in the carriage he dumped his bag beside him. He put his feet up and glared horribly out of the window. A bald old man, unperturbed, got in and went to sit where the bag was. Dan swung the bag up to put it on the rack. Plunk! He hit and smashed a light bulb and bits of glass pattered over the miserable blue suit.

The girl opposite crossed her long legs, lifted one leg to fiddle with the heel of her high-heeled shoe. Past the band at the top of her stocking (re-inforced to give the suspender something to hook into) that inner surface of her thigh was her softest and sweetest part. In a tunnel the train stopped dead. The one bulb gave a bead of light.

"Aren't you frightened?"

She didn't answer. He stretched to get something from his bag. As he did so his army boot struck her leg hard. When the train brought them out of the tunnel he saw the heavy dark mark on her leg caused either by a bruise on the skin showing through the stocking, or by the black polish from his boot. As she got out at the next station, she said to him, in a strong cockney voice: "If you're the kind of a miserable little sod who takes it out on young girls, the sooner you're locked up the better."

The train swung out towards the strange fresh air, rising from a concrete ditch topped by level railings, passing another train sliding in the opposite direction into the long hole: first the head then the long body last the tail light spinning away and down. He looked into the back windows of grey slum houses, grey lace curtains, bits of kitchen, geysers and cupboards. Further from London life got easier. Hundreds of oblong back

119

gardens, trees, television aerials, multicolored clothes on clothes-lines, shirts, upsidedown trousers held by pegs one to each ankle. Outside stations in desirable residential areas massed cars waited: some for wives with spare keys, to do the shopping; others till evening to save their masters ten minute healthy walks. Came odd hopeless triangles of desert: long grass, planks, patches of stinging nettles, pram bits, small hills of gravel; nobody owned them.

A monster black and yellow Army sign shattered the countryside. He obeyed the arrow, walked across open heath, among beach trees and blackberry bushes. The berries were hard and green or having-been-picked with a morose scrap of hay left behind. The kids must be on to them as soon as the green gets tinged with pink. They are forced to eat them hard and sour because if one leaves them as uneatable, others will risk the tummy ache. He dreaded arriving at the camp, pictured it again and again. He remembered the radio blare and the cursing, the purposeless parades, being ordered about by unintelligent Sergeants.

His job was to push trolleys or carry shelves of supplies from the Food Store to the Kitchens. He put both hands under the heavy wood shelves which were piled with loaves, slabs of lard, bacon, bowls of potatoes. His neck muscles and the backs of his knees ached. The trolleys, mysteriously, were always empty, so they were light and easy to push. He liked pushing trolleys best. It was the most useful work he had done since joining the Army.

5

He was downstairs early, before them. The maid on her knees in the lounge was laying the fire, her bare legs stuck out from under her skirt. Among the plates on the breakfast table there were as usual two butter dishes. One, between his father's place and Helen's, held yellow heavy butter. In the other, convenient to his own place, he recognized the white flakiness of margarine. He changed the dishes over. At breakfast he spread the butter thickly, asked for more toast, kept the dish close to him. He smiled at Helen.

His father was calling for him to come out to the car immediately, he couldn't wait all morning, he at least had some work to do. Dan went quickly to the maid's room, stood holding the door open. She sat on the cheap bed, darning her skirt.

"Could you spare just ten bob, Joan?"

"You know I'm not paid till Friday."

"Sorry."

"Wait, I think I have two shillings."

She opened the wardrobe with a little key that had survived three owners and two second-hand shops. While she searched in her handbag, he looked, ashamed, at the bits of worn carpet which didn't match. A porcelain Christ hung from a nail on the wall. Catholic pamphlets and women's magazines were piled up, tattered from being read religiously. She gave him half-a-crown.

"I'll pay you back. It's damn nice of you."

"It's nothing of the kind."

He walked from his father's office to the public library. Intently, he indexed things: a charwoman washing the tiles in the doorway of a chemist's shop, her broken shoe; a cubic yard of white hot coke in a machine thugathugathugathuga making asphalt; a chap looking up at a lorryful of fruit.

At a table in the Reference Library and Reading Room he struggled to study, learned rare words, wrote sexy stories. A tired woman dragged a child to the *Nursing World* in a rack on the wall, hisswhispering:

"Michael I'm not hurting you. Now stop it. I've got you so your hand can't slip."

Situation vacant. *The Law of Master and Servant.* Preface. The author could not forbear to mention the generous assistance afforded him by. A ragged tanned man asked at the counter for the *Bankers' Almanac* please. The librarian, a thin girl with tight curls permanently waved, consulted reference books about reference books.

He said: "It's all right, I'll find it."

She hurried, touched his elbow.

"It's BA 332.8."

She pointed to the shelves.

"I can get it," he said.

He hovered in the middle of the room. Reaching up on tiptoe, she put her hand on a large blue book, tips of her fingers at the top of it, her palm resting the spine. He looked down at her shoes.

"Thanks, I'll get it," he said.

She eased the book out so that a triangle of it was away from the shelf. She walked back to the counter, past him. He stood before the books, reading their heavy-lettered titles. Hummed a bit. His long brown forefinger touched *Bankers*, did not move the book. He took his hand away. He scratched his neck inside his collar. Chapter One: Nineteenth Century. Conditions of employment. The early Workmen's Compensation Acts. Whereas. A girl shook the table as she scribbled hard, notes from the *Encyclopedia Brittanica.* Rubber products. She leaned across the book, resting her bosom on it. As she wrote, the end of her pen, which was soured and scratched where she had nervously sucked and bitten it, jabbed into her rhythmically. He bent down to tie his laces, looked up at her beneath the table. Shadows. KOJE yelled from a newspaper headline. And the prisoners at the gateway sang their international song. "One miner's worth ten lawyers," he had said to Gerson. "Yes," Gerson had replied, "down a mine." He moved to another table, and worked. As he left, at twelve, for lunch, an old lady was explaining to the Chief Librarian: "It was an anthology by Herrington, I have it so firmly in my mind. And so have you, haven't you?"

"I wouldn't say that madam."

"You'd remembered you'd seen it."

"Well I might have seen it on a list."

"Yes, that's right, on a list."

* * *

"Helen tells me you've been borrowing money from the maid again."

His father was tired.

"I'll pay her back."

"That's not the point. It's not nice. And I've given you twenty-five pounds this month. That means you're spending over six pounds a week. Families live on less, and you've got to." "I don't know where it all goes. If you exploited the workers less intensively I might qualify for a government grant, and then I'd be on my own."

"Is that what you want?"

"Maybe it's what many people want."

"You're quite wrong Dan only the other day Helen was saying
—."

"I know; 'how much she liked me'."

Dan heard the kitchen door slam. He said quickly: Saw a loony boy this afternoon."

"Mmm."

"He was making a pig in the sky with string."

Helen jerked the door open. "Perfect timing" he thought. She saw him smile.

"What was that?" she asked.

His father said quickly: "Only a boy Dan met."

"Didn't he say 'pig' or something?" "Yes? There's a marvellous program on tonight. Danny Kaye."

"He's brilliant," Dan said.

"I wonder if he passed his law exams first time." Helen said.

"Well I'm certainly going to, if that's on your mind."

"Of course you are," said his father. "There's time for a cocktail before dinner. Dan, get the ice. Have we a fresh lemon and a little grated nutmeg, Helen?"

* * *

He sat for his exam. It would be a month until the results were published in The Times. He had to do something. Anything. He walked into the *Town Hall.* "I'm forming a branch of the Peace With China Committee," he announced.

"Oh, well —" said the young clerk.

"I'm told you could give me a list of local organizations."

"I'll see."

He called through a door: 'Young gent here from the China people wants the Orgs file."

Mumbles. Squeaks. A cardboard folder.

"Fraid you can't take it away, but you can copy the addresses."

For ten days he knocked on doors, asked Beekeepers, Octogenarians, Pacifists, Conservatives, Folkdancers, Scouts, Labour and Communist Party members, Rose-growers, train-spotters, curates, trade unionists, stamp-collectors, youth leaders, to Stop MacArthur, Prevent International Conflagration and keep their hands off China.

Sixty enthusiasts were invited to the Inaugural Meeting at Dan's home, Thursday evening, 7 p.m. sharp. Helen and his father went early to the cinema. Joan was told she could go after she had prepared the egg sandwiches. Bottles of light ale which his father had ordered from the Off-licence stood in rows on the floor, and on trays tall glasses waited in twelve columns of five. Dan brought down the old Left Book Club books and strewed them around.

At seven, Rickie came, from the big house next door. He was middle-aged, a vegetarian, ran a cycling club for boys; he wore shorts. By seven thirty, two nice old ladies from the Peace Pledge Union were sitting in armchairs talking with Bert a cross-eyed chap in a blue suit with a rucksack. At eight o'clock Bert said they needed a Chairman and would Dan open the meeting. Dan stood by the fireplace, said yes, well they all knew why they had been asked, and if they agreed with the Aims of the Committee they could form a Branch and try to do something about it because it was a mistake to think that the People were powerless. That was playing into the hands of the Reactionaries. The People flew the bombers and fired the guns and the People could make war impossible. They ate sandwiches and Bert drank a quart of beer. They agreed to hold a public meeting in the Church Hall. Bert had some pamphlets about Peoples' China, and they all bought one. They decided to meet monthly at Bert's home. Dan was elected Secretary by four votes to none.

Helen complained about the mess. His father said cigarette ash was good for the carpet, it made it grow, and he told everyone that Dan was Secretary of the Peace Movement.

Dan was still in bed on Saturday morning when Helen brought up the papers.

"I can't find your name in *The Times,*" she said.

"Then I've failed."

"You're very calm about it."

"There's no point in getting hysterical," Dan said.

"What will your father say? You might show some feeling for him, after all he's done for you."

"He's a very generous man. Don't you find that?"

"You're his biggest disappointment—"

"Mind your own business."

"Your father's happiness is my business."

"Quite a profitable one."

"Take that back! Take that back!"

She was crying. He heard her sobbing and shouting in his father's room. He thought, good he's got something else to think about apart from my bloody exams.

His father came in, sat on the bed.

"Do you want to give up law?" he asked.

"Of course not."

"There's no 'of course' about it. You could have passed that exam. You're not a fool. You just didn't work."

"Other chaps fail."

"You're not like them. You can do it, Dan. I only wish I had your chances, I'd be working day and night. I'll help you all I can, but you've got to do the work."

"I could study better in a place of my own. Nearer the College to save travelling."

"All right. I'll find you a room not too far away, so you can come home for the weekends."

The three of them had become expert at mealtime chat, but lunch was like an escalator suddenly stopped, everyone having to climb the unaccustomed stairs. Dan sat quiet, looked at his face upsidedown in a spoon. Helen chatted in little swoops. Up she went, then, hearing the brittle brightness, stopped awkwardly. His father knew the weight was on him, and cautiously avoided forbidden places. He pointed with his knife at the electric clock:

"That was a bad buy, Helen, it's never been right since we bought it."

Helen said: "And the trouble is you never know whether it's going to gain or lose, but our bedroom one is—"

Dan interrupted her: "It's caused by minute variations in the electric current, you know. But that steady sweep of the big hand. It's so impressive. Gets people every time."

He wondered whether they would leave his chair by the table, or put it against the wall. The table was going to be very big for the two of them. Joan brought in three cups of coffee on a green plastic tray. His father glanced from her breasts to the coffee cups and back again.

Dan went to Bert's house, to see about the Committee.

"I'm sorry dear, Bert's not back from work yet," his wife said, "I know he'd like to see you, he's told me about you, come in and wait, I'll make a cup of tea."

She was pregnant, about seven months gone. She shut the front door behind him. "Clack" of a Council house, not "Clonk" like the door of his home. The house seemed as full of kids as she was: four of them, "the eldest is nine", ran around the kitchen, into the garden and back again, up and down the stairs, got legs caught in the banisters, swiped each other with sticks, knocked over milk bottles, pushed a rusty old pram round and round the garden, climbed into the dustbin, got bits of grit in their eyes, used the dustbin lid as a shield while the others threw stones, pulled each others hair, burst into tears, yelled, laughed, wiped dripping noses with greasy hands, sat in a puddle eating dirt, asked questions, painted on the wall *it's our wall*, stood staring at flies, poked a tortoise with a stick, held it up by its shell, screaming:

"Don't drop Mr. Wooby! Don't drop Mr. Wooby!"

"They dropped him once and cracked him," she said.

She walked round all the time, following them, telling them off, listening to Dan, talking to him. The kettle went on whistling. Her belly pushed at him. She had a wheelbarrowful of childbelly, she wheeled it in front of her. He sat harmless on a kitchen chair waiting for her navel to shove into his face. Her belly was covered by a skirt wrapped round it, huge pink and white blobs and big white buttons. The last three buttons hung down by their cotton threads pulled by the kids scrambling beneath her. Like a huge mother sow she didn't crush one of them. She bent down, showing her pink underslip, and wiped or swiped bits of fluff and hair from the kids' sticky mouths, and yellowish snot from their noses.

"Glad to see you here, Dan."

Hefty handclench. He poured himself a cup of tea. Through the cabbagey smell of the kitchen his sweaty smell came over. His wife lifed a baby from a pram in the corner:

"It's time for his bath."

And she pushed herself upstairs. "Been digging trenches in the park," Bert said. "Foundations for a new school. They must have heard about my lot."

"I'm terribly sorry Bert, I've got to give up the Peace Committee." Dan knew he was talking in a special way, slurring words and dropping aitches.

"That's all right mate. Didn't your mum approve?"

"It's not that. I'm getting a flat in town, on my own."

"Well well," Bert said.

6

Unshaved and unwashed because a spider stayed circling shrivelling still crawling round the wash-basin, he lay on the hard bed, looking at the nude on the wall, the blackblistered cold fireplace, the gas ring squatting on the lino. He sat up. Some bright bits on the carpet were spots of daylight from the other side of the earth. Tunnels made by needles. He remembered when Grandma swallowed a needle and a year later it came out of her heel. Faces, camels, goblins, birds lived in the patterned curtains; behind the window but almost flush with it, a darkbrick neighbor wall shut out the night.

He trod down the quiet creaking stairs, got outside. Street lights shone yellow madly at nobody Sky men in purple overcoats and floppy pink hats played moon-football. His nose was cold. Fresh on his face light rain fell. He pounded over the ringing pavement. "Be twenty. Poise dizzy at an angle on a waterfall edge. Look down, see the white gas there. Plunge, splutter, shoot away and race away downriver." Rain fell, bounced, danced, on his pavement which he'd put there on purpose.

He looked in at a workmen's cafe. He wasn't a workman. Water tricked down the misted window, it was warm inside and cold out.

Home, he flopped on the bed. Spider's a long time dying. Up once more, he put the bacon he'd bought into the saucepan he'd bought, watched the warmed fat become lucent, ooze, begin to crackle. He sniffed.

Downstairs again to the lavatory, taking things with him. The slightly slimy stone rim refused his body warmth. He stretched his leg forward, pressed his foot against the door to keep it shut. He read the brownpaper-covered book he had taken from his father's wardrobe. First acne, underwear, the Orient, spiritual awareness, conducive foods: cloves and saffron, black molasses. Then at last, Love-play, Coital Positions, Perfect Courtship, Ideal Marriage, Advanced Coital Positions, Notes for the Obese.

The other book, twisting nudes, lay on the floor. He tried to read the two together. O manufacturers of frosted glass for the windows of suburban lavatories.

The gas ring still flared in the dark room. The bacon was charred dust on the ceiling and out the window, the floor wet with liquid saucepan. He offered himself a saucepan sandwich.

* * *

Helen's precise hand: two neat strokes sliced through the old address and small clear letters announced the new. The envelope contained an Invitation to a party, from Montague.

Frantic in the frantic center of the frantically crammed room Montague stood with his hairy hands in his hairy jacket pockets. Dan walked right up to and on top of him talking immediately loudly continuously. *Quelle savoir faire.* He wore his pipe and Montague told him how well it suited him, made him look much older. Dan joined the homosexual cowboys chatting cleverly at bubbly girls. What do you do? Me Yugoslav partisan — part-time. What's your favorite color eyes? The great eyes of camels and the eyes of men in Sainsburys. He stopped. He'd climbed over himself. Embarrassed girls looked at each other's feet, drifted away. But she circled, dancing, a glance for him each time round. Her northern hemispheres bounced, wobbled, jumped. She looked, double-chinned, down at them, a basketful of puppies. He took her drunk damp hand, let her into the room reserved for sexual intercourse. It was going to be lovely.

He said: "Bell fling float kite cap kiss shell hill plough panther antler elegant bending rainbow rain garden grave—"
"What are you talking about?"
"Just a game."
"Kid's game," she said, "one word leads to another. One two three. We all know that."

His head lay on her lap, he spoke to her tummy.
"Words don't describe, they point, and poets hit the source in history, the shadow behind each word. Don't slip so quick from step to step. Rest. Words are abstract isolate ancient huge, flipping and floating in colored balloons in fanlight air. Yelp. Out it flasht. Flashtitout. Timmy begoodboynow. Guttergone. Autumn eats trees with amazing flames, leaving the indigestible bones for deadwinter."

She stared across at the bodies fiddling and squeezing and heaving.

"Why go on?" she said.

"For the prize, to dirtily prise your knees and thighs, to deliberately split your delicious infinitive."

"Oh. Well you can get off me."

In the main room people sank by stages to the floor, spilling drinks over each other.

"Somebody stole your gal?" Montague asked.

"Seizing abandoned property is no larceny," Dan said.

"So you're going to be Lord Chief Justice after all?"

"Never. My heart's not in it. I don't care who owns things."

"Your father—"

"Forget him. One death was tragic, but two made him ridiculous. Now the weight's on me, and brother he's in for a disappointment."

"Does he ever talk about Bryan;" Montague asked.

"The dirty words in our home are dead wife and dead son. Never mentioned. Not a picture, not a word."

"Because the alternative to silence is a scream?"

"Because Helen's a doll, a real doll, and she mustn't be made miserable."

"If it weren't for her," Montague said, "If you were left alone with him, you'd soon find him hanging by his braces. Your father is living with Helen, and he's alive with her. But you want to camp in galleries of tinted photographs. Why dwell on death?" "Why not wallow in it? Hell how grandma would have wallowed and wailed and bellowed and punched herself blue! With us each emotion is clipped like a privet hedge or a slick moustache. Throw away your lines, be polite, and after two gins be charming. That's all. But I want to learn Latin, be in the desert, kill with an axe, cover my ear in gravy, piss on their carpet, fill that bloody television set with old cod. Ours is not an ikon, it's got doors, it's a triptych. Them, their actual heads and legs I love all right. But they've been suffocated by junk. They can't even cry for the dead."

He belched.

His friend stood up: "You'd better go home."

"It's too early," Dan pleaded, "let's go to the pictures, or—"

"I'm taking you to the nearest Underground."

Alone and singing in a huge lift going down. No, there was a man with him, working the lift, listening, chewing. Two big eye teeth and a thin loose lip, which he chewed. He prodded a bellysoft thumbshape into shadow. A strong spring flung the steel gate across and slammed Dan's ear out.

"Eye teeth!" Dan bawled, "You've knocked my bloody ear out! You and the Senior Lift Operator and the Assistant Station Master and the Station Master and the Designer of Lifts and the Constructor of Lifts and The Minister and Her Majesty and Hieronymus Bosch and the Bishop of Bath and Wells. And I'm gonna boot the lot."

Carefully he balanced on one foot, gave a quick swing and kicked himself out onto the non-slip floor. Eyeteeth picked him up, leaned him against the tiled wall and told him he'd had a drop too much. Scraps of rag and paper lay in the lift hole, cables and weights and wheels moved steadily. Miles above, a metal voice cried:

"Stand Clear of the Gates".

Two hundred times a day he used to yell that, yelled himself hoarse. Now he does a new recording once a year and switches on whenever he wants. Dan saw three sharp little black studs with clear silver letters: nonsec; bel; bug. He tried to hang on to the smoothtiled wettish wall.

Suddenly he was deep in people rushing on and off and anyhow. Crowds of girls, a porter with a watering-can, soldiers, boys in striped scarves, actresses, dreary gentlemen. He swam along. He was going home.

* * *

They dined in the Temple, formally, on benches, enclosed by ancient coats of arms, by King Charles tiny and pointed on his thirty foot cart horse, a gorgeous woodcarved ceiling, stained glass windows scarlet and ultramarine, pockmarked servants, a macebearer with a mace, glossy collars and cuffs and teeth pinpointed against dark suits and the solid brown of panelled oak. Montague, Dan's guests, was impressed.

"When I went into my Dad's dress business," he said, "I never knew what I was missing. Twelve hundred a year and the night plane to Rome when the peaches are ripe is all very well, but this, this is Big, Dan. It's grand, it's historical, it's feudal. The yanks should make a color film of it."

"You ain't seen nothin' yet," said Dan. "Here comes the Procession of Judges. Something to tell the grandkids."

The line of old men doddered along between the tables, near close enough to touch. The Senior Judge thanked the Lord beautifully for His bounteous liberality and everyone sat down.

"Man, they're the ancientest," said Montague.

"They are indeed incredibly old, and diseased," said Dan. "And

131

remember that I, if I sweat and strain, I may become one of those."

"It's a great incentive," said Montague. "Look at that little one, he's fantastic. Those facial muscles, that premature bulldog look. How does he do it?"

"Each morning." Dan replied, "after gargling, he informs the bathroom: 'I, Mr. Justice Presley, Enshrine the Constitution. I have never heard of rock and roll'. He repeats this to his wife who says: 'Yes dear'. He pulls on his long pants, eats a very big breakfast, is conveyed to the Courts, where, robed and throned, ten miles above the multitude, he tells workingclass witnesses to 'Speak up man!' because he can't hear a word."

"Seriously," said Montague, "what makes you so bitter?"

"Tell me why in all history a Judge has never once said: 'Put a sock in it', 'Fuck you Jack', 'My leg itches', 'I feel awful', 'You look a lovely bit of stuff'?"

"I'll answer your question if you answer mine."

"I failed my exam."

"Again?"

* * * * *

"You have proved that Property Law is a swindle and therefore not worth studying," his father said, "but you failed Divorce too?"

"Divorce is as big a fraud as marriage. Let people do as they please. They're grown ups. Live-together or not-live-together. Who cares?"

"The children?"

"Farm them out to mass-crèches supervised by trained male nurses."

His father was counting pound notes from his wallet. "Here's ten pounds," he said. "Make it last two years."

"Did you discuss this with anyone we know?"

"Don't be stupid, Dan. Why didn't you work? If you were a bloody fool I could excuse it, but you're just drifting. Life's been too easy for you. You need a shock. If only I had my time over again . . . I got to London with a five pound note in my pocket and a wife and child in the back of the car."

"You had a car then?"

"You know what I mean, Dan."

"Yes I do."

132

"You think you do. You heard about the young man of nineteen who thought his father an idiot, and at twenty-one he couldn't understand how—"

Dan chimed in the last words: "— the old man had learnt so much in the last two years."

They smiled.

"I mean it Dan. When I was your age I worked from six in the morning till twelve at night. Sometimes drove up to Lincoln to fetch a big load, then a quick turn round and down to the Garden by early morning. The other firms had drivers, but I was on my own. We lived on sandwiches, that's what ruined my digestion."

"I thought it was booze."

"I did things then I'd never do now. I'm old."

"You're a success. You're well off. You've built up a business. You smoke cigars and drink whisky. You've a beautiful redhead and a 21 inch T.V. What more do you want — ulcers?" "I was born at the wrong time. Ten years earlier and I'd have made a million. But those days will never come back. There isn't the money to be made any more, not that kind of money. I remember them coming to me with the first idea for football pools, but I'd been caught too often."

"So you're rich and successful and full of regrets. Why can't you understand when I say my heart's not in it?"

"Who gives a damn if your heart's not in it! My heart's not in it! Go to your beloved workers on their way to work in the morning, if you can get up that early, and ask them if their hearts are in it. You'll get some funny answers."

"Then what's the point of it all?"

"The posing of that question is a luxury you can no longer afford. You can start worrying about philosophy when you are in a steady job."

7

He found Montague seated in his maroon upholstered swivel chair, using his two white daily-sterilised telephones, consulting his stainless steel filing cabinet, blinking at graphs, confiding in his suedette secretary, fiddling with the thermostatically-controlled central heating system. Fitness for function. Montague's function was to meet foreign buyers, note carefully that they were all unable to state precisely the quantity and quality of the goods they wished to import, and to have lunch every day with Dad and the other Directors. He was unable to spare Dan a few minutes, lend him four pounds, and give him a note of introduction to Max Spencer, an appeals organiser for charities, who required an assistant secretary with a public school background.

Spencer carried a yellow glove in his yellow-gloved hand. Dan had worked for him for a fortnight, and was learning to keep a special boyish grin for the Chairmen of the various Committees, to create an attitude rarely cringing, yet always sufficiently deferential.

"I wonder, Graveson, whether you could take the Minutes for the A.O.'s tonight," Spencer asked.

His tone of voice implied: although I speak jauntily, this, young man, is your chance to prove yourself.

Dan's navy suit and blue and gold old school tie contrasted with the virgin whiteness and special glossiness of a brand new Van Heusen collar style eleven. He travelled by taxi to the Mayfair address. A pretty starched white and bright blue maid opened the fine front door:

"May I take your coat sir? The A.O. meeting is in the front lounge sir. Thank you sir. This way sir."

Three chaps in middle-aged sports jackets sipped sherry together. Dan stood close to the wall holding the cardboard file Spencer had given him. He walked over to the table, took a glass of sherry from the silver tray, felt himself in the middle of the room.

More people came: ladies with expensive legs, company directors who looked like company directors, talking together of maids and motorcars.

"Mr. Graveson?"

The hostess beckoned to him.

"Have you everything you need? A pen? Do use this card-table for your papers."

Like a Jane Austen curate he sat straightening his papers while the guests finished their sherry and slowly settled elegant bottoms in elegant chairs.

In a cultured voice Dan read the Minutes of the last meeting at which it had been decided that the Ninth Annual A.O. Ball should be held at the Saveloy Hotel. The meeting then proceeded to the discussion of the main item on the agenda: the question of prizes for the Tombola. The chairman of a whiskey firm offered a case of whisky as first prize. He was congratulated, thanked, held up as an example. "Simply splendid," said the treasurer, "if we had a few more Gerald Felthams all our problems would be solved."

The price of Tombola tickets was debated passionately. Finally a compromise motion referring the matter back for decision by the Annual Ball Tombola Sub-committee, was carried by eighteen votes to nine with eleven abstentions. The treasurer estimated that the Tombola should make approximately two hundred pounds profit.

"What's that in terms of A.O.'s?" he asked Dan.

Dan read from the illustrated leaflet:

"Two and sixpense will buy enough dried milk to maintain an Asian Orphan in good health for approximately five days."

"Simply splendid," the treasurer said.

Dan didn't go to Spencer's office the next morning, or ever again. Spencer wrote, at first politely then rudely, asking for the return of his A.O. file.

8

Multilith operator, Adrema embosser, accounts clerk, upholsterer, Burroughs P600 operator, invoice checker, delivery man, marine engineer, Capstan lathe operator, warehouseman, stove enameller, reinforced concrete engineer, window dresser, pig man. He was none of these. He wasn't even a Hairdresser's Assistant. Two columns of vacancies for shorthand typists. He bought a Teach Yourself Shorthand book, explained to the landlady that as soon as he got through it, say twenty-four hours solid work, he would be earning at least ten pounds a week. He reached Chapter Three.

He was thrown out of his room. Bodily. There's the rent and the state you leave your room in it's not nice the smell and tins everywhere the bed unmade dust all over sink blocked up it's not nice for the other tenants not that they've complained but it's not nice. Be out by morning. He wasn't. Her brother came. Headbutting bastard. Armwrenched body-buffeted buttock-bumped bullied and socked downstairs and out.

Bums in lines queued for jobs and thirty bob odd doled out by clerks from behind heavy wire.

"Report three times a week to get your card stamped."

To make sure you've not got a job same time as you're collecting. Dan waited all morning between tough blokes, Irish and Jamaican. Didn't talk to them. Shuffled up as queue moved forward. One bloke bounced on his toes, swinging a violin case so that everyone knew he was not an ordinary bum but a musical bum.

By hungry lunchtime Dan found out he was in the Manual Labour queue. Bricklayer's assistants only.

"All right, I'll take that."

No son, you've got school certificate. Come next Thursday, ask for the clerical department."

He walked down streets, strange ones. Camden Town. He sat on a seat placed on a triangle of grass between busy roads. Good to sit down, lots to look at. Bless the Victorian philanthropist. Then women carrying shopping gooped at him.

Parkwandering, somewhere, he set a deckchair on its feet, wiped the birdshit off, sat. Got up, altered the back strut, sat again, more stretched out, nearer the ground. An attendant tinged close by. He leapt up, sat on a wooden seat, a free one. Nowhere to sleep. Lucky it was warm.

He went to the free lavatory. The door was lower than the penny lavs. He moved with bent knees so that his head should not be seen. A spade and two brooms were kept there. One broom soft for dust, the other, thick copper red spines wet with disinfectant. No pick-up seat; only a rim of stained wood. Advertisements for venereal diseases. A metal notice above an empty box: *Toilet paper must be obtained from the Attendant.* A tramp with dirty bum must hobble out and ask for paper, please.

He found a sheltered place to sleep, protected from the slight evening wind. He took off his jacket, bunched it into a pillow, lay his cheek on it. Shivered. Picked up a fallen log for a pillow. Beetles. Flung it away. Stood still. Bells rang ArangArangArang. "A-a-a-a-1 Out! A-a-a-a-a-a-a-a-1 Out!"

Hide. Down quick on his knees in the leaves, heart bumping. No. He got up, brushed the earth off his clothes, ambled out of the main gate. It was damp and cold now.

Raw noise. Tens of thousands of wheels on roads. Heaps of persons, hives of them, pouring from and into buildings, crowding up steps from underground, crouching in cars, stopping in the street gaping at gadgets in windows, getting pinched elbowed killed drunk dazed, reading evening papers, obeying policemen, selling (and buying) fruit. He bored through them, out to Holbon and the dead City where the daytime moneymagnet was switched off and it was empty. Greenish light lay on the windows of banks, insurance houses, tobacconists. Policemen shone square lights at doors, and tested locks.

Blitz sites. He was walking with conscious leverage from leg to leg. His legs weighed impossibly heavy. He came to a thudding hellplace, gleams of fires, men swung shovels, the ground shook, it was between mountains.

"What's happening?"

"Government contract. Double shifts."

The steepening road grew bendier, slummier. Tramlines whipped away, shining. He looked at the headlamps of cars spinning round roadbends, coming and going, like spies signalling, but not to him. Asphalt now, to fall and cut your knee on. Everyone's got a scar on his knee from falling off a bicycle or something, onto a gritty road; an inch of blue grey dead. The regular street lights passed him one to the other. He was lit by two lights making two faint shadows; the third substantial shadow where the two overlapped, had an inhuman shape. Tremendous lorries bound for Glasgow Strasbourg Benghazi thundered past him onwards paralysing as panzer divisions. A dog barked. Bing beng, quarter past something. He found a nameless place with smashed windows and swinging door and a man on a backless chair. He crept in, lay on the floor, felt his head and spine against stone. His feet swing high and round and round in gorges, canyons.

Slammed in the ribs by boulders:

"Out you get, out of it. Railways property. Out with you. Come on out of it."

Very slowly the morning sun warmed him. It was going to be another fine day. He stood with his back to a lamp-post, turned his face into the sun for a moment. He'd ended up at Billingsgate of all places. The insane fish smell drove him up the hill, spitting. He passed a dead bus stuck in a hole, and early workers whistling.

"Ullo Ken, 'ow yer going"?'

"Can't complain."

He had been here before, ages ago, with his father. He found a halfpenny on the pavement. A kid pointed at his shoe: "Look mum, it's got it's mouth open."

Policemen glanced at him.

He finished the tea and the ham roll and walked slowly to the door.

"Not so fast. That's tenpence."

"So sorry. I clean forgot."

He felt in his trouser pockets. Halfpenny. He looked intently into his wallet. An old woman pushed in, past him. A wrinkled stick from an Irish hedge, crimson hair tangling from under her hat which had berries on it. She hooked her man's umbrella on to the counter, and in a sharp Belfast voice asked for a cup of tea. But the man looked past her:

"Well?"

"I haven't a penny on me," Dan called from the door, keeping his grip on the handle. "Now what do we do? I'm really most dreadfully sorry. A cheque for tenpence, of course, would be ridiculous."

"Buzz off. Go on, get moving. And don't come this way again in a hurry. I'll know your mug for next time."

He had to get decent. He got back to his father's home, knowing his father would be at work in the afternoon. Helen came to the door, wiping her hands on her apron.

"Dan! What a state you're in! So that's how you've been carrying on. I thought you were meant to be studying." "I'd like some lunch please."

"It's half past three. Nearly tea-time."

He shoved past her into the kitchen. She followed, stood holding the door. He opened the fridge, took out a bottle of milk, a cold roast chicken, a carton of potato salad.

"That's your father's supper."

"He'll understand."

"But there's nothing else in the house. What am I going to tell him? What will he say?"

They stood over him.